THE TRACTION LIBRARY

WANT EVEN BETTER RESULTS AND MORE BUSINESS SUCCESS?

IT TAKES YOUR WHOLE TEAM.

Every person on your team must be equipped with the right information and tools to implement EOS, the Entrepreneurial Operating System®, purely throughout your organization. With The Traction Library, your entire company—from leadership to management to employees—will understand their role and be better equipped to help your company succeed.

HERE'S HOW!

AVAILABLE BOOKS	WHO IT'S FOR
Traction	For everyone
Rocket Fuel	For the Visionary and the Integrator
Get a Grip (*Traction*'s fable)	For the leadership team
How to Be a Great Boss	For leaders, managers, and supervisors
What the Heck is EOS?	For all employees, managers, and supervisors

Visit **www.eosworldwide.com** to get everything you need to fully implement EOS in your company today.

WHAT THE HECK IS

EOS?

A Complete Guide for
Employees in Companies
Running on EOS

GINO WICKMAN
& TOM BOUWER

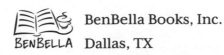

BenBella Books, Inc.
Dallas, TX

The EOS Model™, The V/TO™, The Meeting Pulse™, The "Level 10" Meeting™, The Issues Solving Track™, The People Analyzer™, GWC™, The EOS Process™, The Six Key Components™, The 8 Questions™, Core Focus™, and 3-Year Picture are trademarks of Gino Wickman. EOS® and The Entrepreneurial Operating System® are registered trademarks of Gino Wickman. All rights reserved.

BenBella Books, Inc.
10440 N. Central Expressway, Suite 800
Dallas, TX 75231
www.benbellabooks.com
Send feedback to feedback@benbellabooks.com

Printed in the United States of America
10 9 8 7 6 5 4 3

Library of Congress Cataloging-in-Publication Data is available on request.
ISBN 9781944648817
e-ISBN 9781944648831

Editing by Glenn Yeffeth
Copyediting by Ginny Glass
Proofreading by Michael Fedison and Sarah Vostok
Text design and composition by Aaron Edmiston
Graphic design by Drew Robinson Spork Design
Front cover design by Faceout Studio
Full cover design by Sarah Avinger
Printed by Lake Book Manufacturing

Distributed to the trade by Two Rivers Distribution, an Ingram brand
www.tworiversdistribution.com

To place orders through Two Rivers Distribution:
Tel: (800) 343-4499
Fax: (800) 351-5073
E-mail: IPSJacksonOrders@ingramcontent.com

To Kathy, my partner in life. You are real, you are fun, and you are beautiful. Thank you for being you. What a ride the first 30 years have been; can't wait for the next 30.
—Gino

To Sev, my amazing wife. I would be less than complete without you. Your strength, intelligence, and ability to light up a room with positive energy are only surpassed by your incredible compassion.
—Tom

Contents

INTRODUCTION

We've written this book for you because you play a critical role in your company's success and, therefore, your own—because your success and your company's are deeply linked.

Whether you are a customer service rep, accountant, field-service rep, salesperson, sales-support staff, welder, truck driver, architect, consultant, or any other role, this book was written to help you be more successful in your company—a company running on EOS (the Entrepreneurial Operating System).

So, what the heck is EOS?

CHAPTER 1
WHAT THE HECK
IS EOS?

Your company is using EOS (the Entrepreneurial Operating System) as its "operating system."
So, what the heck does that mean for you? Before
answering that question, it's important to first
understand that every company has an operating
system, whether it has a name or not.

That system is the way a company organizes all of
its human energy. It's the way that the people in the
organization meet, solve problems, plan, prioritize,
follow processes, communicate, measure, structure, clarify roles, lead, and manage.

It's hard to understand the operating systems of most companies because the leadership teams aren't consistent in how they do the above. This inconsistency leads to poor communication, dysfunction, and employees feeling frustrated and confused about what the priorities are. Ultimately, the company never realizes its full potential.

The reason you're reading this book is because your leadership team wants everyone in your organization to understand how EOS works, to see the value of its structure, and to help them implement it.

Why one operating system? The short answer is that everyone doing it their own way in an organization can't work. You can't have a company where everyone can set the priorities, meet the way they want to meet, and use different terminology.

If you have 50 people doing everything 50 different ways, the increased complexity leads to mass chaos. Even worse, people experience incredible confusion and frustration. Simply put, you can't build a great company on multiple operating systems—you must choose one.

For instance, at an IT services company in Atlanta, every project was managed differently because each project manager led their project their own way. When employees moved from one project to the next, they had to learn a whole new project management system with different reporting, status updates, and meeting structures. As a result, they wasted a lot of time trying to learn a new system—time that should have been spent serving clients. Due to this inconsistent approach, people grew frustrated, and the company started losing clients, employees, and money.

The truth is, a team of average people running their company on one operating system will outperform a team of high achievers, each doing it their own way, every day of the week. That is why your company needs a clearly stated operating system that everyone follows.

WHY EOS?

So, why this operating system? Because it works. More than 50,000 companies all over the world run on EOS. It's a complete, simple, and powerful operating system. It helps companies grow to achieve their vision and goals more effectively.

It also gives the employees of those companies a well-defined structure in which they can grow, feel more fulfilled in their work, and achieve their personal goals. It helps them feel more "in-the-know" about what's going on. When you understand what the priorities of the company are, it helps you play your part in achieving them.

As Kathleen Watts, an account manager at PMMC, put it, "Before EOS, I didn't have a lot of insight into the bigger picture. Communication from management was not streamlined. Now we're much more aligned as an organization, and I know what we are trying to do and how I can help."

EOS also saves time. When everyone in your organization is rowing in the same direction, you'll find that you are communicating better. EOS eliminates unhealthy and time-wasting activities due to miscommunication. Down the road, that means avoiding train wrecks that can cost your company tons of money and cause you lots of headaches.

At a Connecticut technology firm, meetings would go for hours and hours without anything ever getting resolved. The CEO said, "Once we implemented EOS, we stopped wasting time with unnecessary meetings. We're getting more done and are communicating more effectively with our employees. They've told me that as a company, we make a lot fewer mistakes and now solve problems before they become major disasters."

EOS AND YOUR LEADERSHIP TEAM

EOS is specifically designed for a 10 to 250 person entrepreneurial company that is open-minded and growth-oriented. In our experience, this is where EOS has the most impact. While it works for companies larger and smaller, this is the true sweet spot for EOS.

As a part of implementing EOS, you will notice that the leadership team of your organization goes off-site occasionally for full-day working sessions. They do this to get 100 percent in sync and on the same page with one another. When away from the office, they work hard to solve all of the high-level issues facing your company and to set quarterly priorities. This ensures that the entire organization can stay laser-focused on achieving your company vision.

Business is hard—that's reality. With constantly changing technology, competition trying to crush you, and demanding customers and clients, your leadership team has to wrestle with 136 issues at any given time. They can't succeed without great people throughout your organization. They can't do it without *you*.

EOS AND YOU

It's also important that *you* know you can't do it alone. You need a team that you can depend on and that can depend on you. If you've been thinking, "What's in it for me?" that's fair and understandable. The short answer is that EOS will help you to work more effectively, with less frustration and a clearer understanding of the connection between your efforts and the success of your company.

As one employee said, "EOS helped me really understand where I fit in the company and how I impact everyone else. We have a great team, and it is fun to work here."

You may be thinking that implementing EOS in your organization sounds rigid, will stifle creativity, and will rob you of your uniqueness. Actually, just the opposite happens. Just as a computer's operating system is an underlying framework that helps you be more productive, EOS will do the same for you and your organization. Its underlying framework will magnify your unique contribution and help you be more productive.

So now that you know why your company is implementing EOS, let's begin the journey, because that's what this is. EOS is not a project with a specific end date. Implementing EOS in your company is an ongoing, lifelong effort. Many companies have been running on EOS for more than 10 years.

To start the journey with your company, first you need to understand the big picture, which we will describe in Chapter 2. Then, in Chapters 3–7 we will share the 5 foundational tools that form the backbone of EOS. Finally, in Chapter 8, we will share a few bonus tools that will be the icing on the cake.

CHAPTER 2

HOW DOES EOS WORK?
(THE EOS MODEL)

My first impression was that EOS was
just another management "thing."
It's not. EOS really works.

—JOEL TALLEY, business development,
Nexus Health Systems

Now that you know why an operating system is so important and why your company chose EOS, the next step is for you to understand how EOS works.

Every company is comprised of 6 Key Components. This chapter will give you a high-level view of these components. You'll see why each component is important, and how EOS strengthens each component. You'll also discover how they impact you.

The 6 Key Components (Vision, People, Data, Issues, Process, and Traction) are illustrated in the following EOS Model.

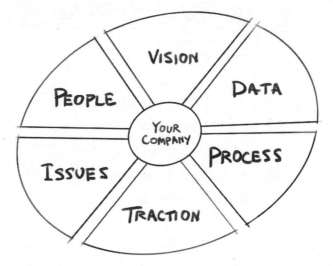

By using EOS to strengthen these 6 Key Components, your company will be a great, well-run organization. Your company's goal is to be 100% strong in each of these areas.

The EOS journey is not easy. You will have to challenge yourself, your manager, your team, and your company. That's because open and honest communication throughout the organization is a requirement. Most importantly, in the EOS system you must play an active role in strengthening each component.

If you've ever felt you are "just an employee" or that you don't have a voice, that is simply not the case with a company running on EOS. A company running on EOS wants you to push, pull, and prod to help get each component as close to 100% strong as possible.

Now, let's get a high-level view of each component and an introduction to the tools you'll be using to become 100% strong in each one.

THE VISION COMPONENT

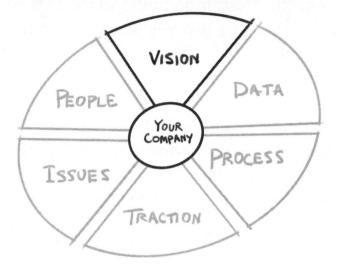

Have you ever been given direction from your manager only to be told something different by a leader from another department? If you answered yes, you're not alone. This is a common problem in many organizations.

It is caused by a lack of alignment within an organization. In other words, each manager or department has different priorities and does things differently. As a result, employees get pulled left, then right, and then told to go backward.

Imagine all the people in your company as arrows. When people have different objectives, the arrows all point in different directions, as shown in the picture below. As a result, energy is wasted.

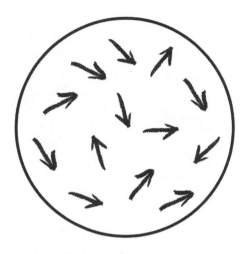

This was happening at a transportation company based in Houston. "Before EOS, I would get told one thing by my manager and another thing by the owner of the company," said one of the customer-service reps. "We were running around in circles, making the same mistakes again and again."

Now imagine the people in an organization that are 100% aligned around just a few goals. Everyone's effort is focused toward accomplishing these few goals. Each department and every employee know the roles they are playing to help achieve these goals. As a result, the arrows are aligned, as depicted below.

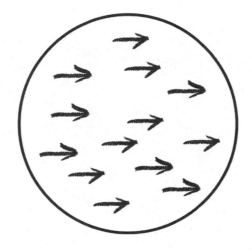

"Now," continued that same customer-service rep, "we all have the same goals, and we've worked together to solve some major issues. Our efforts are aligned, and I know what I need to do to help achieve our vision. Even better, we've stopped repeating the same mistakes."

That's being 100% strong in the Vision Component. When everyone in the company is working toward the same goals, there is less frustration and fewer mistakes. More gets done in less time, and work is more fun. As one employee exclaimed, "WOW! We used to never hit deadlines (if we even had them). Now we are very focused and get a lot more done. Everyone's priorities align."

There are a handful of EOS tools that are used to strengthen the 6 Key Components. The EOS tool used to strengthen the Vision Component is called the Vision/Traction Organizer, or "V/TO." It helps everyone in your company get aligned on the same short-term and long-term goals. The V/TO asks the organization, from the owners to everyone throughout the company, to have the same answers to 8 simple questions. This tool will be explained fully in Chapter 3.

Your role is to understand and buy in to the answers to these 8 questions and to know where your organization is going, where you fit in, and how you can help.

THE PEOPLE COMPONENT

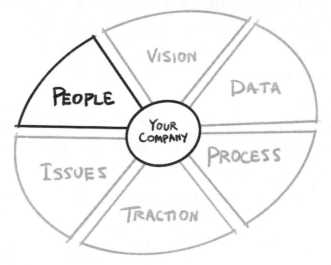

Have you ever had someone on your team who just didn't fit? Maybe they caused problems between other people by gossiping or backstabbing. Perhaps they were really nice but just couldn't do the job, causing others more work.

If this sounds familiar, you probably found it maddening. The People Component eliminates that problem. It helps build great teams. It puts the Right People in the Right Seats.

The Right People are the ones who just fit. You know them when you see them; you feel it. They are people you like to work with, people who, like you, want to accomplish something every day. They sacrifice so the team can win. They act according to a code of behavior: your company's Core Values. These are the Right People.

The Right Seat means getting everyone in a role where they can best contribute to the organization: A job where they can be successful. A place where they can accomplish something every day. A person in the Right Seat is someone who consistently excels at a clearly defined, necessary job in the organization.

Imagine your company with 100% of the Right People in the Right Seats. Work is done more efficiently. There are fewer fires to put out. Mistakes are rare, and communication is better. The company grows, creating more opportunities for everyone. It is truly a great place to work.

"Our teams work more closely together because we have the Right People in the Right Seats. We work through problems in a timely manner with better service for our clients," stated Jordan-Ann Schorch, an account manager at Syrup Marketing.

For the People Component, companies use 2 EOS tools: the Accountability Chart and the People Analyzer. We will explain these more in Chapters 4 and 8. Your role is to ask yourself, "Am I the Right Person for this company? Do I fit?" and, "Am I in the Right Seat? Can I do my job really well?"

THE DATA COMPONENT

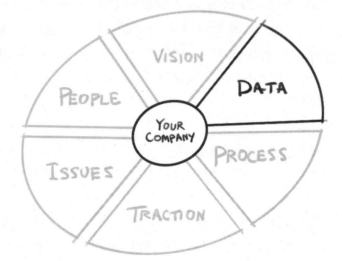

Would you ever get on a plane with no control panel, no gauges, and no radar? Probably not. Yet that is how many companies operate. They fly blind every day. They can't see where they are going because they don't have the right data—sometimes too much and often too little.

The Data Component is designed to help you objectively see where you are going—both as an individual and as a company. It eliminates assumptions, subjective opinions, emotions, and ego. The 2 EOS tools that will help your company become 100% strong in the Data Component are Scorecards and Measurables.

A Scorecard has a handful of numbers that, at a glance, tell you how you are doing and where you are going. Your company's leadership team reviews the company Scorecard weekly to always have a pulse on the business, to make sure everything is on track, and to identify issues so effective action can be taken. Your department or team should also have a Scorecard.

For example, a Houston-based ship repair firm tracks weekly job bids in dollars. When the total weekly bids fall below $400,000, they know they need to take action, or they will not have enough work in 4–6 weeks.

Myra Ebarb, director of human resources at Sachse Construction, said, "Scorecards allow us to focus on numbers that drive the business. The

Scorecard keeps track of progress at all levels of the company, and we now know when action needs to be taken."

A Scorecard contains Measurables, which are numbers for which someone is accountable. For example, you might track customer sale meetings, units produced, the days to close the books, on-time shipping, or utilization. Ultimately, every employee in the company should have a Measurable and a goal for that number.

Why? First, so you objectively know how you're doing. Second, so your manager knows what you've accomplished. Third, so your team keeps a pulse on where you are and if you are on track for where you want to go. It will also help you identify small problems so you can solve them before they become a major crisis. We will fully explore Scorecards and Measurables in Chapter 7.

Your role is to look objectively at your job and department and come up with Measurables. At first look, it might surprise you—you might not be doing as well as you think you are. On the other hand, you might be doing great and not getting the credit. Either way, don't worry; by using Scorecards and Measurables, you'll know if you are on track to achieve your goals.

THE ISSUES COMPONENT

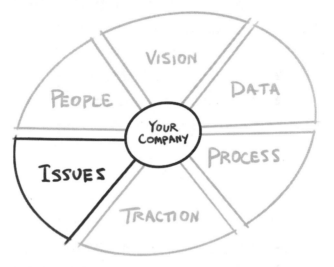

By now you've probably thought of a few things that need to be improved, fixed, or changed to make your company better. These are called issues. They include anything unresolved that needs to be discussed, such as problems, opportunities, or new and better ways to do things.

Perhaps you see an issue or a way to make things faster. Perhaps you see a way to do things more easily, to sell more, to reduce rework or mistakes, or to fix the inventory problem—a way to do your job better.

So, how does your organization solve these issues? You might have just thought that they don't. If so, you're not alone. Many companies discuss issues . . . and discuss them . . . and then discuss them some more . . . but never solve them. This leads to finger-pointing, dysfunction, and frustration for both managers and employees. Why? Because nothing ever is resolved.

Here's the good news: it doesn't have to be this way. The Issue Component is designed to help your organization bring issues to the surface and solve them, once and for all. As Kelly Imhoff, a marketing manager at Staley, Inc., put it, "I now have a place to raise issues that impact me—and they actually get solved. I participate in the process, so I have a lot more buy-in to the decisions."

The 2 EOS tools that strengthen the Issues Component are the Issues List and the Issues Solving Track. The Issues List allows everyone to openly and honestly list all unresolved issues. The Issues Solving

Track is a disciplined way to help you prioritize and solve issues forever. More on these tools in Chapter 6.

Going forward, your role is to bring up the issues you see—and to help solve them. If this sounds scary, that's normal. If this makes you nervous, you are not alone. Rest assured: EOS will give you the tools to safely and effectively do this. If you accept this role, you will help make your company great.

THE PROCESS COMPONENT

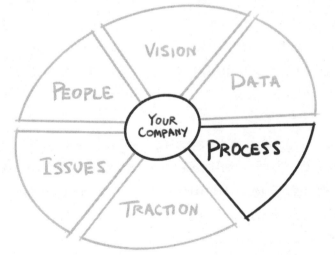

Do you manage projects in different ways? Do sales people enter orders in different ways? Do people take equipment or materials and then fail to replace them? Are you constantly chasing the same information each month?

If so, this indicates a lack of standard processes. The Process Component creates, at a high level, a consistent way of doing all the company's operations. It is basically a checklist.

Imagine everyone taking tools and then putting them back in the same place. Picture all projects being managed the same way. Consider every sales order being entered the same way with the same information. Following the same process saves an incredible amount of time and eliminates a lot of frustration. It helps you perform your job with fewer mistakes, delays, and expenses.

As part of implementing EOS, your company's leadership team will document the company's Core Processes. These include the way you make your product or provide your service from A to Z. It covers the way your salespeople sell your product or service—from generating leads all the way to closing the deal. It streamlines the way that you serve your customers so that they are satisfied every time. It standardizes the way your company bills, collects, and manages money.

When the Process Component is 100% strong, your organization has documented the core things you do every day. Everyone follows these processes, creating consistency and efficiency. Even better, these processes can be scaled so that your company can grow in a manageable way.

Your company will systemize all of the predictable and redundant tasks so you can use your creativity to solve problems. In other words, when processes for repetitious tasks are uniform, your energy can be put toward the unexpected. When this happens, your area will start to run like a well-oiled machine.

Your role is to learn and follow the company's Core Processes as well as to objectively look at how you are doing things each day. Ask yourself: What are you doing that is unnecessary? Are you doing something because one time 5 years ago a customer complained and you're still doing it today? What is the best and most efficient way to do your job?

THE TRACTION COMPONENT

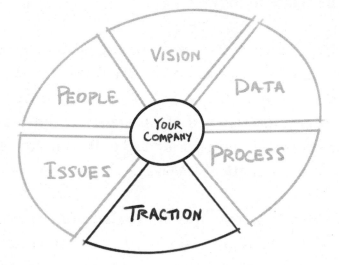

Are people in your company accountable? Do things get done on time, or are due dates constantly missed? Does your company take on too much? Has your company been trying to implement a software system for years and the project just never seems to end?

This was the case for Velocity Productions, a video production company in the Southeast. They had been trying to implement new accounting software for more than a year. "We just couldn't finish the project," said one accountant. "It went on and on—we didn't have any traction."

You may be able to relate to that scenario. Now, picture an organization where projects get completed on time and people who commit to a deadline hit it. They don't want to let one another down, so they put in the extra effort needed. Imagine if your meetings began and ended on time. What about a company where people don't make excuses and unproductive people can't hide, so they leave? Or, where everyone focuses on only a few priorities for the next 90 days—and those priorities are tied back to the company's overall goals? Things just get done.

Strengthening the Traction Component will create the organization described above. It is about discipline, execution, and accountability. It helps a company clarify and choose the right priorities. When the Traction Component is 100% strong, you get . . . Traction!

Brad Sovine, ecommerce manager at Uckele Health & Nutrition, said, "Our company is more structured. Meetings are more efficient. We now work more as a team and focus on the most important objectives. Everyone knows exactly what their priorities are and has a clear path on how to achieve those goals."

The 2 EOS tools used to strengthen the Traction Component are Rocks and the weekly Level 10 Meeting. We address these in detail in Chapters 5 and 6.

Rocks are 90-day priorities—the most important things you need to get done in the next 90 days. The weekly Level 10 Meeting lays down an agenda so you solve issues and stay connected as a team. These 2 tools help your company be more disciplined and execute better.

Your role is to set Rocks with your manager every quarter and to complete them on time. Your role is also to be fully engaged and actively participate in your weekly Level 10 Meetings by helping to identify and resolve issues.

CHAPTER SUMMARY

So now you know why you need an operating system, why your company chose EOS, and what your company looks like when each of the 6 Key Components are 100% strong.

Everyone in the company will be rowing in the same direction. You will have great people throughout the organization. Measurables will be in place so you have a pulse on where you are in relation to your goals. All issues will be solved quickly. Everyone will follow the Core Processes, creating consistency and scalability. You will execute well, with clear priorities and highly productive meetings. Everyone will work together as a healthy, cohesive team, ultimately making your company's vision a reality. It will truly be a great place to work.

"EOS is like mental health for a business," commented Doug Hebert. "Everyone is much more engaged, feels more united and part of the team. EOS brought us together as one team. People appreciate the increased communication and transparency. It heightens the level of engagement, and I have a clearer picture of what we're doing."

Another employee had this to say about the effects of EOS on his company: "We now have a team of people pulling the rope in the same direction. This has helped the company and everyone working here be more successful."

You probably noticed that the description of each component ended with your role: basically, what's expected of you. Here's a short recap:

Component	What's it all about	Tool(s)	Your Role
Vision	Getting everyone aligned and focused on the same vision	V/TO	Understand and buy into the answers to the 8 V/TO questions
People	Getting the Right People in the Right Seats	Accountability Chart, People Analyzer	Ask yourself if you are the Right Person in the Right Seat
Data	Measuring performance and having a pulse	Scorecard, Measurables	Establish and achieve your Measurables
Issues	Identifying and solving issues	Issues List, Issues Solving Track	Bring up and help solve issues
Process	Documenting the way you do things and being consistent	Documented Core Process	Learn, follow, and help improve the Core Processes
Traction	Accountability, discipline, and execution	Meeting Pulse, Rocks	Complete your Rocks and engage in meetings

Now, we know that's a lot, and we're only 2 chapters in, so let's put your mind at ease—you don't have to do everything by tomorrow. Most companies take a minimum of 24 months to strengthen each of the 6 Key Components. So your patience and commitment will be needed, because once you are at 100%, it is a lifelong commitment to keep your company there.

Before we dive into each of the tools in the following chapters, here are some questions to ask your manager. We'll list 3 questions like this at the end of each chapter to help you push your company to fully implement EOS.

Questions to Ask Your Manager

1. What is our weakest component, and how can I help strengthen it?
2. What is our strongest component, and why do you think that?
3. What is the first thing you want me to do to help implement EOS at our company?

CHAPTER 3

DO YOU SEE WHAT THEY ARE SAYING?
(THE VISION/TRACTION ORGANIZER)

I always thought management didn't know where
we were going. If they did, they sure weren't
sharing it with me. The V/TO changed that.
**—LINDSEY CLEMENT, accounting and HR
specialist, Proximity Systems, Inc.**

Great companies have leaders who communicate a crystal-clear Vision to the entire company. A company's Vision, simply put, is a matter of defining who you are, where you are going, and how you will get there.

Do you know your company's Vision for the future? Every company has one, but it might not be written down or shared with everyone. Perhaps only a few leaders carry it around in their heads.

A worse problem is when a leadership team thinks they all agree on the same Vision and they really don't. If they don't agree with one another on the same Vision, they and the company will end up rowing in different directions. In addition, when the Vision is not written down, it is difficult for a leadership team to know if they are on the same page—not to mention sharing it with everyone else in the company. This leads to poor communication, confusion, and wasted effort.

As an example, the leadership team members of a New England telecom firm were asked to write down the company's top priorities for the next year. Not a single answer was the same. One person thought that sales were the top priority while another thought it was hiring additional operations people. Yet another manager thought it was opening an office on the West Coast. Clearly, they were rowing in different directions and communicating different priorities to the employees.

The EOS tool that helps your leadership team define, document, agree on, and share the company Vision is called the Vision/Traction Organizer or "V/TO." The V/TO is illustrated on the next two pages.

The V/TO aligns your leadership team around the answers to 8 essential questions about your business. Those questions are shown in the 8 shaded sections in the V/TO. Once your leadership team answers each question, the answers are captured in the appropriate section.

The V/TO helps the team get their vision out of their heads and down on paper so it can be shared with the whole company. Once everyone throughout the organization shares the same vision, they can row in the same direction. They can now "see" where they are going.

Have you ever tried to navigate in a new city without your GPS device or phone? If so, you probably had a good map so you wouldn't get lost. A clearly defined vision shared by everyone in the company is like having that map. It helps you see where you've been, where you are, and where you are going. The

THE VISION/TRACTION ORGANIZER™

THE EOS MODEL™

ORGANIZATION NAME:

VISION

CORE VALUES	1.
	2.
	3.
	4.
	5.

| CORE FOCUS™ | Purpose/Cause/Passion: |
| | Our Niche: |

| 10-YEAR TARGET™ | |

MARKETING STRATEGY	Target Market/"The List":
	Three Uniques:
	1.
	2.
	3.
	Proven Process:
	Guarantee:

3-YEAR PICTURE™

Future Date:
Revenue: $
Profit: $
Measurables:
What does it look like?
• • • • • • • • • • • • • • • • • •

THE VISION/TRACTION ORGANIZER™

ORGANIZATION NAME:

TRACTION

1-YEAR PLAN	ROCKS	ISSUES LIST
Future Date: **Revenue:** $ **Profit:** $ **Measurables:**	**Future Date:** **Revenue:** $ **Profit:** $ **Measurables:**	
Goals for the Year: 1. 2. 3. 4. 5. 6. 7.	**Rocks for the Quarter:** Who 1. 2. 3. 4. 5. 6. 7.	1. 2. 3. 4. 5. 6. 7. 8. 9. 10.

result is a stronger company, which leads to more job security and opportunities for employees.

Now that you understand why getting everyone on the same page with your company's Vision is so important, we'll next take you through a deeper dive into each of the 8 questions on the V/TO:

1. What are your Core Values?
2. What is your Core Focus?
3. What is your 10-Year Target?
4. What is your Marketing Strategy?
5. What is your 3-Year Picture?
6. What is your 1-Year Plan?
7. What are your Rocks?
8. What are your Issues?

We'll now briefly explain why each question is important to you and how each question helps your business unite around its Vision.

QUESTION 1: WHAT ARE YOUR CORE VALUES?

Core Values are a timeless set of guiding principles. There are typically just a few—3 to 7 is the rule of thumb. They define the behaviors you expect from each other. They

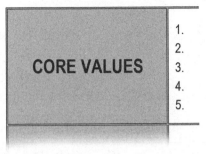

define your culture and who fits and who doesn't. They define what makes your company different and unique.

A famous business guru, Peter Drucker, is attributed with the saying, "Culture eats strategy for breakfast." History has shown that culture wins in the long run, not strategy. For a company to be great, it must first know who it is. Then focus on strategy. Who you are as a company is defined by your Core Values.

Every company has different Core Values because, well, every company is different. To help build a strong culture, your company will use your

Core Values to hire, fire, and review everyone (how this happens will be detailed in Chapter 8).

Here is an example of the EOS Worldwide Core Values (keep in mind yours will be different):

1. Humbly Confident
2. Grow or Die
3. Help First
4. Do What You Say
5. Do the Right Thing

Let's take one of those, "Do What You Say," as an example. In a "Do What You Say" culture, everyone delivers on time. That means if you commit to a date, you hit it. You fully deliver and finish what you start—doing things half-assed or half-finished is unacceptable. Everyone takes responsibility, owns their projects, and blames no one if something doesn't get finished. Finally, in a "Do What You Say" culture, it is okay to say no—if you can't do it, don't commit.

Your leadership team has worked very hard to discover what your company's Core Values are in order to build an amazing culture. Once these Values are shared, we urge you to ask questions in order to fully understand them. Ultimately you have to ask yourself, "Do I share these Core Values?"

You'll find that when you work with people who share the same Core Values, communication is easier, things get done faster, and the work environment is more fun. You will have a great organization and a strong culture.

QUESTION 2: WHAT IS YOUR CORE FOCUS?

Whereas Core Values define *who* you are as an organization, Core Focus defines *what* you are. Core Focus is about 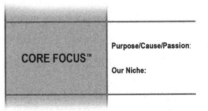 keeping your company and all of its people focused on the areas where your business excels.

It is very easy for businesses to get distracted by "shiny stuff"—things that look like the right thing to do but are really not in the sweet spot of what you do as an organization.

A furniture manufacturer in Wisconsin, for example, spent so much money on advertising each year that they decided to save money by opening their own advertising agency. They spent a significant amount of time and money starting up this division. Unfortunately, in the end, they lost hundreds of thousands of dollars and had to close down the operation. Why? It was not what they did best. Their sweet spot was manufacturing furniture.

Lisa Fisher at United Paint made a comment regarding the power of Core Focus: "Before EOS, we attempted to be everything to everyone, from paint for office furniture to paint for plastic toys in McDonald's Happy Meals. Honestly, if it was a current customer who had a nonautomotive job or a really *shiny* opportunity, we tried it. After EOS, we were able to get to *one* Core Focus—automotive interior coatings for plastic. Shiny stuff is now just not even considered."

Core Focus keeps companies from getting distracted. It comes from the intersection of knowing *why* your company exists and *what* you do in the world.

Your *why* is known as a Purpose, Cause, or Passion. It is an overriding belief that is bigger than a goal, and it makes you want to get out of bed every day. Your *what* is known as a  Niche. It defines the space in which you do business; it identifies what you do better than anyone else. Once these 2 truths are clarified and put together, you have your Core Focus.

Here are some examples to help you better understand Core Focus:

MARKET TRADERS—teaches people how to successfully trade foreign currency
Purpose: Changing lives through empowerment
Niche: Trading and investment education

NEXUS HEALTH—runs post-surgery hospitals
Cause: Returning patients to lives of productivity and meaning
Niche: Specialty health care

TEL AID—helps companies implement large system and IT projects

Passion: Making the complex simple and repeatable

Niche: Large IT projects

Once you know your company's Core Focus, you'll realize that you are part of something bigger than yourself. Hopefully, this will be inspiring. In addition, your Core Focus serves as a filter that allows your organization to say no to good ideas and yes to great ones. As a result, all effort, people, systems, processes, and even products will be designed and aligned to keep you true to what you do best and propel you toward your vision.

QUESTION 3: WHAT IS YOUR 10-YEAR TARGET?

Now that you know *who* you are and *what* you are as an organization, you need to determine where you are going. The 10-Year Target is your long-term, larger-than-life goal. It unites everyone around one common

objective. In many cases, it helps you and your company achieve goals you never thought possible.

Imagine a sailboat without a rudder. It just goes wherever the wind blows it. Many companies are like this—they don't have a long-term target. They don't know where they are going.

Why is the 10-Year Target important? As Yogi Berra said, "If you don't know where you're going, you'll end up someplace else." In other words, if you know where you want to go, you have a much better chance of getting there.

In addition, working toward a long-range goal can create more opportunities for employees like you. Finally, it gets everyone asking the right questions, like: What does our company need to start doing differently to reach our 10-Year Target? What do we need to change? What could we do better?

These examples will help you better understand the 10-Year Target:

Company	Current Reality	10-Year Target
ExCargo – A cargo transportation company	25,000 containers moved a year	112,000 containers moved a year
Velocity Productions – An AV and event company	$6 million in revenue	$20 million in revenue
LSR Multi Family – A roofing company	No roofs on the moon	Roof the first apartments on the moon
Autumn Associates – An insurance agency	Not getting enough referrals from clients	A referral from every client and every client from a referral

With a clear 10-Year Target that is shared by all, you will have a guiding light by which everyone can steer. This focus will direct your energy, resources, and decisions to help you grow faster and reach your 10-Year Target more quickly.

As with the above examples, most 10-Year Targets involve rapid and significant growth, which can't happen without the right Marketing Strategy—and that leads us to the next question on the V/TO.

QUESTION 4: WHAT IS YOUR MARKETING STRATEGY?

Defining your Marketing Strategy requires crystallizing who your ideal customer is and clarifying the most appealing message to them. Doing this will create a laser-like focus for your sales and marketing efforts. This in turn will help increase your sales and move you toward your 10-Year Target.

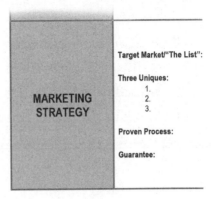

MARKETING STRATEGY

Target Market/"The List":

Three Uniques:
1.
2.
3.

Proven Process:

Guarantee:

You've probably had to deal with a customer who is a pain in the butt. They call your service department multiple times a day for the wrong reasons. They submit special orders that fall outside your standard process. You fix computers, and they want you to fix their desks.

Many companies waste thousands of dollars trying to be everything to everyone. They waste money with inconsistent marketing messages. They take sales trips to prospective customers who are never going to say yes or are not a good fit for the company. They commit to projects in which they have no expertise.

The Marketing Strategy will help you stay focused, selling to customers who are the most receptive and take less organizational time to service. It will help align your organization around the real, unique value you provide the customer.

Your Marketing Strategy is made up of 4 key elements:

1. Target Market
2. 3 Uniques
3. Proven Process
4. Guarantee

Let's take them one at a time.

Target Market

The Target Market identifies the characteristics of your best customers (who they are, where they are, and how they think). Once your Target Market is identified, your company can focus more energy toward those ideal customers and less toward others who don't fit or who generate less profit. Here is an example of a Target Market:

- $5–$50 million in revenue
- 20–250 employees
- Southeastern United States
- Growth-oriented
- Seeking a partner, not a commodity provider

3 Uniques

The 3 Uniques describe the 3 things that make you better than the competition and why your customers buy from your company. For example, they could be the following:

- 99% on-time delivery
- Local technicians
- 24-hour response time

Proven Process

The Proven Process is a visual of what you do, time and time again, to deliver value to your customer over the life of the relationship. It creates a picture of what your customers will experience when they work with you. Here is the EOS Proven Process:

Guarantee

Your Guarantee is designed to take away your customers' biggest fear when it is time for them to buy. It says that you stand behind your product or service. This is where you put your money where your mouth is. Here are 3 different examples that companies have used:

- We will hit our ship date, or we will pay for your shipping.
- If we don't add value, you don't pay.
- We will show up on time, or the first hour is free.

These 4 elements make up your Marketing Strategy. Once implemented, you will focus on customers who are easier and more enjoyable to do business with. Your 3 Uniques will provide a consistent message for all of your sales and marketing efforts. You will differentiate yourself and put your clients' minds at ease with your Proven Process and your guarantee. All of these will help increase your

THE EOS PROCESS™

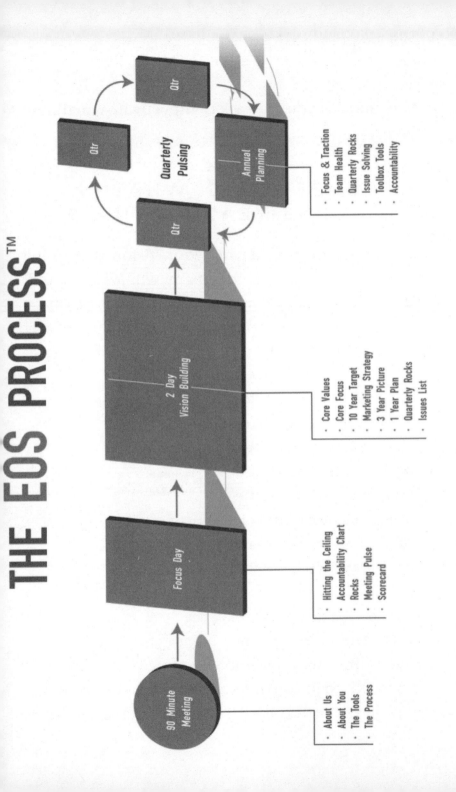

90 Minute Meeting
- About Us
- About You
- The Tools
- The Process

Focus Day
- Hitting the Ceiling
- Accountability Chart
- Rocks
- Meeting Pulse
- Scorecard

2 Day Vision Building
- Core Values
- Core Focus
- 10 Year Target
- Marketing Strategy
- 3 Year Picture
- 1 Year Plan
- Quarterly Rocks
- Issues List

Quarterly Pulsing

Qtr   Qtr   Qtr

Annual Planning
- Focus & Traction
- Team Health
- Quarterly Rocks
- Issue Solving
- Toolbox Tools
- Accountability

sales and put you on track to hit your 10-Year Target faster.

QUESTION 5: WHAT IS YOUR 3-YEAR PICTURE?

The next step in achieving your Vision is painting a picture of what your company will look like in 3 short years. The 3-Year Picture creates a vivid image of exactly what your company will look like, feel like, and be like in 3 years.

Unfortunately, a lot of managers don't share their picture of the future with employees. Why not? Most of the time, they don't know it themselves—or at least haven't written it down.

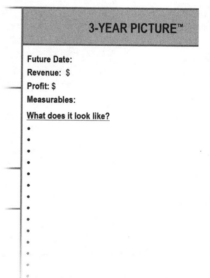

The 3-Year Picture helps everyone see the same image 3 years down the road. It contains just a handful of numbers: Revenue, Profit, and a Measurable. In addition, it contains 5 to 15 bullets that "paint" the picture for you. Here is an example of a company's 3-Year Picture:

Date: 12/31/20XX
Revenue: $14.5 million
Profit: $1.8 million
Measurable: 300 customers
What does it look like?
- 80 employees
- 3 new product lines
- 100% Right People in the Right Seats
- Bright, energetic, fun office
- Strong culture
- Largest customer accounts for <10% of revenue
- Best place to work in the state
- All Core Processes documented and Followed By All

The 3-Year Picture allows your leadership team to paint a powerful picture of the future so you can see what they are saying. Once everyone sees this Vision, it is more likely to happen. It's important that you ask questions once this is rolled out. By challenging anything that isn't clear, you will ultimately understand the big picture and then decide if you want to be a part of it.

Once clear, it will give you the context in which to set goals for the next 12 months. Which leads us to the next question.

QUESTION 6: WHAT IS YOUR 1-YEAR PLAN?

This is where we start to take the Vision down to the ground. A solid 1-Year Plan makes the goals more tangible. Simply put, your 1-Year Plan defines your objectives for the year. It identifies and crystallizes your revenue target, profit target, and a Measurable, along with your top 3 to 7 goals for the year.

1-YEAR PLAN

Future Date:
Revenue: $
Profit: $
Measurables:

Goals for the Year:
1.
2.
3.
4.
5.

Why only 3 to 7 goals? Because fewer is better and less is more. When companies try to get too many things done, they lose focus and, as a result, accomplish very few of them. With too many goals, organizations spread resources across too many priorities and then fall short.

One company in New Jersey drew up 15 priorities for the year. "We tried to get all of them done, but in reality we accomplished very little," stated the CEO. "We just spread our people too thin. Now we pick 3–7 goals for the year and have been very successful at accomplishing most of them. It's one reason our sales increased 18% this past year."

Once your 1-Year Plan is clear, you'll know exactly what you need to accomplish over the next 12 months to put you on a path to reach your 3-Year Picture and ultimately achieve your 10-Year Target. All energy and resources will be focused on your selected few goals, propelling your company forward and providing you with a greater chance of success.

Here is an example of a company's 1-Year Plan:

Date: 12/31/20XX
Revenue: $8 million

Profit: $900,000
Measurable: 150 customers
Goals:
1. Sign deals with 2 premier vendors
2. 100% Right People in the Right Seats
3. Add 3 salespeople to the current team of 7
4. All Core Processes documented
5. Add 50 new customers

Hopefully, you see the pattern, from the 10-Year Target to the 3-Year Picture down to the 1-Year Plan, which helps everyone know what's most important in the coming year. And that will create the clarity necessary to set your quarterly Rocks.

QUESTION 7: WHAT ARE YOUR ROCKS?

Rocks are the 3 to 7 most important objectives the company must get done in the next 90 days in order to achieve your 1-Year Plan.

Why 90 days? In most cases, companies start the year with good intentions, but then life gets in the way. In January and February, everyone is energetic and focused on the priorities, but then people start getting distracted by competitors' actions, unplanned emergencies, and day-to-day distractions.

ROCKS	
Future Date: Revenue: $ Profit: $ Measurables:	
Rocks for the Quarter:	Who
1.	
2.	
3.	
4.	
5.	
6	
7	

As a result, that great energy is lost, and plans start to unravel and fray. Deadlines get pushed back, and priorities get lost in the hustle and bustle. All of a sudden, November rolls around, and you're saying, "Oh crap! How are we going to get this all done?"

Rocks help solve this problem by breaking down annual goals into bite-size chunks. This approach is illustrated in the following story:

On January 14, 2015, Tommy Caldwell and Kevin Jorgeson finished one of the most difficult climbs in the world—the sheer southeastern face of El Capitan in Yosemite National Park. They spent 19 days scaling the almost 3,000-foot, *never*-before-free-climbed vertical wall. When asked how they did it, Jorgeson said, "We've been working on each of these stages and climbing 'pitches.' [We broke them] up by rope lengths. Our ropes are about 200 feet long, so the pitches are obviously 200 feet long or less."

In other words, they climbed the 3,000-foot face 200 feet at a time. To reach their overall goal, they broke it down into smaller, manageable chunks by setting short-term goals along the way.

Another benefit of Rocks is that they create a 90-Day World for your organization that addresses an important aspect of human nature—human beings tend to lose focus, get off track, and fray about 90 days into any project. Rocks get everyone refocused right on the 90th day as the unraveling begins, avoiding the coming fray and maximizing everyone's efforts and energy.

Here are some examples of company Rocks:

Date: 3/31/20XX
Revenue: $2 million
Profit: $200,000
Measurable: 115 customers

Goals:
1. Fill one sales position
2. Software version 2.3 in production
3. Go/no-go decision made on new office
4. Purchase 4 trucks

By setting Rocks every quarter, your company will get a lot more done in a lot less time. Every 90 days, your company will refocus and set new Rocks. With that done, everyone will know the most important priorities for the company every 90 days.

QUESTION 8: WHAT ARE YOUR COMPANY'S ISSUES?

The final question is as important as the previous 7. To achieve your company's Vision, it is vital to openly admit all of your company's obstacles to the opportunities that lie before you. This is simply a list of all the things that could prevent your company from reaching your Vision or that will help you get there faster.

ISSUES LIST
1.
2.
3.
4.
5.
6.

All organizations have issues. The problem is that, in many companies, no one admits them, or when they do, everyone just talks about them but does nothing. As a result, it feels as if there are hundreds of problems that are never resolved.

At the furniture manufacturer in Wisconsin who false-started with the ad agency, employees were asked to list the issues they saw. The following is an actual conversation:

> EMPLOYEE: There's a hole in the roof of our
>   warehouse.
> CEO: So how big of an issue is it?
> EMPLOYEE: Every time it rains or snows, water
>   drips on the furniture, and we have to
>   throw the furniture out.
> CEO: How much money did that cost us last
>   year?
> EMPLOYEE: About $250,000.
> CEO: That's 20% of our profit!
> EMPLOYEE: Yeah, we've been talking about it
>   for a year.

Putting all of the issues on one list will help your company get a handle on them. And remember:

in addition to problems, issues are also ideas and opportunities. You might have an idea on how to grow the company faster. That idea must be added to the Issues List too.

Once the issues are out in the open, the EOS tools in the following chapters will help you to prioritize and solve them. Once your issues are listed, your company can start to prioritize and work them one at a time—resolving them forever. The first step is admitting them.

So now you know the 8 questions that make up the V/TO. You should have a good idea of what each means and why they are important. When completed, your organization's V/TO will look similar to the example on the next two pages.

If you haven't seen your company's V/TO yet, your leadership team will probably be sharing it with you soon. Please note that some companies roll the V/TO out to employees all at once and others roll it out one piece at a time—either way is fine. Also, you can ask your manager if your company's V/TO is ready to be shared with you.

THE EOS MODEL™

THE VISION/TRACTION ORGANIZER™

ORGANIZATION NAME: ABC Company

VISION

CORE VALUES	1. Humbly Confident 2. Grow or Die 3. Help First 4. Do The Right Thing 5. Do What You Say
CORE FOCUS™	**Passion:** Deliver value with every interaction **Our Niche:** IT Solutions
10-YEAR TARGET™	$50 Million in Revenue by 20XX

MARKETING STRATEGY	Companies with: revenue between $5 - $50 million;
	Target Market/"The List": 20-250 employees; growth oriented; seeking partners
	not commodity providers; in the United States.
	
	Three Uniques:
	  1. 99% On-Time Delivery
	  2. Local Technicians
	  3. 24-Hour Response Time
	
	Proven Process: The ABC Proven Process
	
	Guarantee: We'll show up on time or the first hour is free.

3-YEAR PICTURE™

Future Date: 12/31/20XX
Revenue: $ 14.5 million
Profit: $ 1.8 million
Measurables: 300 Customers

What does it look like?
- 80 employees
- 3 new product lines
- 100% right people in the right seats
- Bright, energetic, fun office
- Strong culture
- Largest customer accounts for <10% of revenue
- Best place to work in the state
- All Core Processes documented and Followed by All

THE VISION/TRACTION ORGANIZER™

THE EOS MODEL™

ORGANIZATION NAME: ABC Company

TRACTION

1-YEAR PLAN

Future Date: 12/31/20XX
Revenue: $ 8 million
Profit: $ 900k
Measurables: 150 Customers

Goals for the Year:

1.	Sign deals with two premier vendors
2.	100% right people in the right seats
3.	Add three salespeople to the current team of seven
4.	All Core Processes are documented
5.	Add 50 new customers
6.	
7.	

With your cursor in the last row, press Tab to add another row.

ROCKS

Future Date: 3/31/20XX
Revenue: $ 2 million
Profit: $ 200k
Measurables: 115 Customers

Rocks for the Quarter:

		Who
1.	Fill one sales position	
2.	Software version 2.3 in production	
3.	Go/No Go decision made on new office	
4.	Purchase four trucks	
5.		
6.		
7.		

With your cursor in the last row, press Tab to add another row.

ISSUES LIST

1.	EOS Rollout
2.	Operations Lead
3.	S.E. Territory Sales
4.	3rd Product Line
5.	Training Program
6.	
7.	
8.	
9.	
10.	

With your cursor in the last row, press Tab to add another row.

CHAPTER SUMMARY

Once your leadership team answers the 8 questions and your V/TO is complete, documented, and shared with the entire company, you'll have a crystal-clear picture of who you are, what you are, and where you are going as an organization. You'll ultimately have a great company filled with great people who fit your Core Values. Your Core Focus will serve as a filtering and guiding mechanism for deciding on people, products, customers, and processes.

All effort will be aligned toward achieving your 10-Year Target. Your Marketing Strategy will focus your sales efforts on the right clients with the right message. Everyone will see, buy into, and work toward the 3-Year Picture.

Shorter term, all energy will be focused on achieving a handful of goals for the year. Your 1-Year Plan will be broken down into Rocks that will create a very focused and productive 90-Day World. Finally, all company issues will be placed openly and honestly on the Issues List, so you can pick them off by prioritizing and solving them, one at a time.

With this clarity, everyone will be rowing in the same direction. You will be part of an incredibly focused organization with a strong culture.

Sarah McNulty, account manager at Limbach, stated, "We all have a clear idea of what the future goals and Vision are for the company, which helps us remember that our daily activities are focused on a much bigger, future picture. It allows us to realign our activities when necessary to keep us on track."

Here's a summary of each of the 8 questions on the V/TO and what each answers for your company:

V/TO Question	What it answers
Core Values	Who you are
Core Focus	What you are
10-Year Target	Where you are going
Marketing Strategy	Which potential customers you are targeting with what message
3-Year Picture	What you will look like in 3 years
1-Year Plan	What your goals are for the next 12 months
Rocks	What your priorities are for the next 90 days
Issues	What will stop you or get you there faster

Your role is to understand and believe in your company's Vision (answers to these 8 questions) and to align all your efforts toward helping achieve that Vision. You can't do that without asking questions, so to help you do that, discuss the following 3 questions with your manager.

Questions to Ask Your Manager

1. How can our department help achieve the company Vision?
2. What role do I play in achieving the Vision?
3. What is our greatest challenge in achieving our Vision?

CHAPTER 4
WHO'S DOING WHAT?
(THE ACCOUNTABILITY CHART)

The Accountability Chart helped us know
who is doing what and who is responsible
for what. Previously, there was a lot of
overlap, which caused a lot of confusion.
**—DANIELLE HICKS, account
services, Design at Work**

Picture an organization with 35 people where roles and responsibilities are unclear. No one is quite sure who is accountable for what. The result is people all tripping over each other. Everyone working hard but running in circles, accomplishing very little despite all the effort. Deadlines and opportunities are missed. Frustration is high, and everyone is blaming everyone else. With all the finger-pointing, you have to wear eye protection so you don't get poked in the eye. This is the picture of an organization lacking an Accountability Chart.

Great organizations define and implement the *right* structure (simplest and best) that will most effectively deliver their products or services to the customer. It also helps them manage their growth to the next level.

The right structure creates a well-functioning and healthy workplace where communication flows easily. Great organizations clearly communicate this right structure to the entire company so everyone understands where they fit into the big picture and how they contribute to achieving the company's vision.

The right structure will:

- Clarify roles and responsibilities so that accountability is clear.
- Create clear reporting lines.
- Facilitate efficient decision making and problem solving.

- Help people know who to work with to get things done.
- Enable communication flow.
- Identify all of the available seats in the organization.

THE NEED FOR STRUCTURE

When companies start out and have only a few people (fewer than 10), the all-for-one-and-one-for-all approach is okay. This is normal in a start-up when people must wear many different hats to help the company survive.

However, as companies mature (more than 10), they reach a tipping point when this all-for-one approach becomes a roadblock to growth and people start tripping over each other. Everyone is still trying to do everything, and that just doesn't work anymore. The company stalls, sales stay flat, pressure and stress increase, and then the blame game starts.

Why? Because no one knows who's responsible for what, and no one is held accountable for anything. One person described their company in this state: "There were too many cooks in the kitchen."

As an example, you miss a customer deadline, and everyone starts pointing fingers, because there were so many people involved in hitting the deadline. Or you lose a major customer, and 4 different people have 4 different versions of what happened. No one has ownership or accountability. The fact is, if everyone is accountable, then no one is.

When accountability and reporting structure are unclear, people don't know who to go to with questions or concerns or to solve issues. It is pure chaos, communication is a mess, and everyone is frustrated.

THE ACCOUNTABILITY CHART

The Accountability Chart is the EOS tool companies use to illustrate the right structure. It is a super-charged organizational chart that, in addition to showing structure, clarifies the roles and responsibilities of everyone in the organization. It eliminates multiple and often confusing reporting lines between managers and employees.

Further, it establishes clear ownership and accountability for everything that must get done in your company. It crystallizes your company's structure so that everyone knows who is doing what, who is responsible for what, and who reports to whom.

"The Accountability Chart helped me understand where I fit in the bigger picture and what everyone else is doing," said Doug Hebert, a graphic artist at Savage Brands.

What makes an Accountability Chart different from a traditional organizational chart is, first, there are no dotted lines (dotted lines mean an employee reports to multiple bosses, which causes confusion). Second, for each seat in the company, 5 or so bullet points clarify the major roles of that job (as shown below):

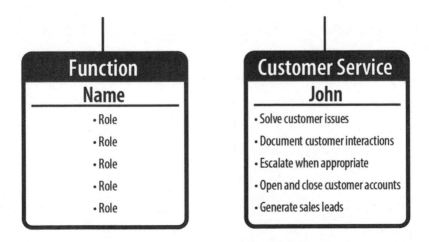

When the Accountability Chart is complete, every seat in the company will be defined with clear roles and responsibilities. Because every organization is different, no 2 Accountability Charts will look the same. There is no "right" answer, there is only the right answer for your company based on your size, growth goals, culture, product, or service. On the next page is an example of a company's complete Accountability Chart.

SCALABILITY

If you haven't seen your company's Accountability Chart yet, your leadership team will probably be sharing it with you soon. You can also ask your manager when it will be ready.

You will notice in the example on the following page, the Field Tech seat doesn't have a name, only "7 People" in it. This represents the number of people in that seat performing the same function. The purpose of the Accountability Chart is not to show all the names in an organization but, instead, all the functions, or "seats" as we like to call them.

The intention is to show how different job functions can be scaled. That way, as your company grows, the Accountability Chart doesn't need to. If you illustrated every name in a 200-person company, you'd need a gigantic document, because 200 seats and names would have to be included.

EVOLUTION

The Accountability Chart is a dynamic tool that is always evolving. It is intended to help your company anticipate structural changes needed to get to the next level. As companies grow, this ability to adjust is critical—structures, roles, and responsibilities will need to change. In fast-growing companies, the Accountability Chart may change as often as every 90 days.

In one case, an oil-and-gas company in Calgary, Alberta, grew from $20 million to over $140 million in revenue in just 4 years. As organizational complexity increased, their Accountability Chart evolved every 90 days to accommodate the explosive growth.

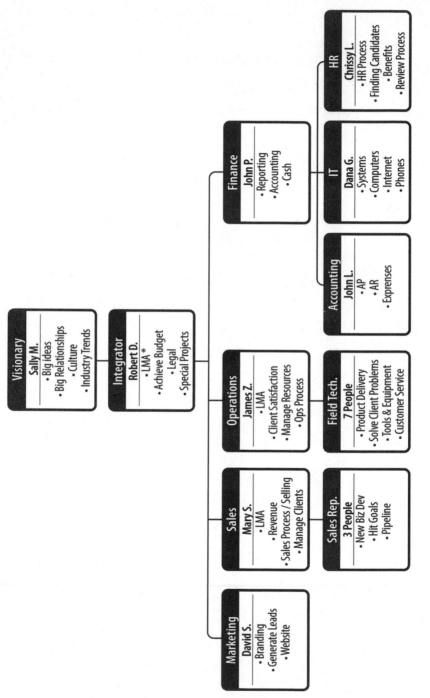

Visionary
Sally M.
- Big Ideas
- Big Relationships
- Culture
- Industry Trends

Integrator
Robert D.
- LMA *
- Achieve Budget
- Legal
- Special Projects

Marketing
David S.
- Branding
- Generate Leads
- Website

Sales
Mary S.
- LMA
- Revenue
- Sales Process / Selling
- Manage Clients

Sales Rep.
3 People
- New Biz Dev
- Hit Goals
- Pipeline

Operations
James Z.
- LMA
- Client Satisfaction
- Manage Resources
- Ops Process

Field Tech.
7 People
- Product Delivery
- Solve Client Problems
- Tools & Equipment
- Customer Service

Finance
John P.
- Reporting
- Accounting
- Cash

Accounting
John L.
- AP
- AR
- Expenses

IT
Dana G.
- Systems
- Computers
- Internet
- Phones

HR
Chrissy L.
- HR Process
- Finding Candidates
- Benefits
- Review Process

* LMA = Leadership, Management, Accountability

When clear roles have been established, you may see some changes in your organization. People may change seats or even leave. Don't worry: this is actually a sign of your company getting stronger, healthier, and achieving its goals. In fact, you may even have the opportunity to change seats as the organization grows. It is impossible for a company to grow from 10 people to 200 people without major structural and people changes. In order for a company to survive, it must remain agile and flexible.

As Joel Talley in business development at Nexus Health Systems said, "I was asked to change my seat. I moved into a seat that fits what I do best, to use my unique skills. This has significantly changed my career path in a very positive way."

COMMUNICATION

While the Accountability Chart clarifies roles, responsibilities, and the reporting structure, it does *not* define your communication structure. In no way should the Accountability Chart create silos or divisions within the company. As shown in the following illustration, communication should flow freely across all lines and departments, creating an open and honest culture. The Accountability Chart should help people know who they need to go to or work with to get the job done.

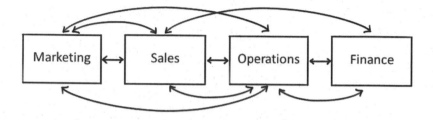

Kevin Polachowski, scheduler at Burkard Industries, described communication at his company this way: "Before EOS, there was a lot of 'go talk to this person' or confusion about who to talk to. After EOS, everyone now knows who to talk to about problems they may have instead of going to several different people and wasting time. Communication flows openly between departments. There are no more silos."

CHAPTER SUMMARY

With your Accountability Chart complete, you will have the right structure to lift your company to the next level. You'll know the roles and responsibilities of everyone in the company as well as all of the "seats." It will be clear who to go to for help or with questions. You will also know whose eyeballs to look into when there is an issue in a specific area of the company.

Open and honest communication will be flowing freely across departments, and you will be solving issues and making decisions easier and faster. There will be greater ownership and accountability throughout the organization. Most importantly, you'll know where you fit in the bigger picture and how you contribute to the overall Vision of your company.

As one employee summarized it, "Now, everyone's roles are defined, and people know what they are responsible and accountable for, which has increased the level of trust throughout our organization and greatly improved our communication."

Your role is to know your seat and where you fit in your company's Accountability Chart as well as to understand and fulfill the responsibilities of your role. To help with that, ask your manager the following 3 questions.

Questions to Ask Your Manager

1. What seat am I in, and what are my 5 roles and/or responsibilities?
2. Am I in the Right Seat, where I can contribute the most to the organization?
3. What are your 5 roles and/or responsibilities, and how can I help you?

CHAPTER 5
WHAT IS MOST IMPORTANT RIGHT NOW? (ROCKS)

> I realized we function best when we have 90-day Rocks. People have short attention spans. When you go longer, things just fall off, and you think you are going to get it done, but you never do.
> **—THERESA DENARO, accounting, CMEEC**

In Chapter 3, we explained the concept of Rocks—the 3-7 most important things that your company must get done in the next 90 days. There, we only talked about *company* Rocks. Now it is time

79

to talk about *your* Rocks—the most important things that *you* must get done in the next 90 days.

How will Rocks apply to you? How will they help you do your job better? How will they help increase accountability throughout your organization?

The term "Rocks" comes from a simple science experiment made popular by Dr. Stephen R. Covey in his book *First Things First*. It works like this—imagine you have a small pile of rocks, some pebbles, and some sand. Your objective is to get them all to fit in a glass jar. If you put the sand in first and then the pebbles, the rocks don't fit (see the jar on the left side of the picture).

However, if you put the rocks in first and then the pebbles (which filter down between the rocks) and finally the sand (which filters down between the rocks and the pebbles), it all fits in the same size jar (as shown in the jar on the right).

The jar represents all the time you have in a day. The rocks represent the most important things you must get done, the pebbles represent your day-to-day responsibilities, and the sand represents all the interruptions during the day. The point is, if you don't prioritize your Rocks—and work on the most important things first—you will not get them done.

As Kevin Polachowski, scheduler at Burkard Industries, stated, "Before we had Rocks, projects were often talked about, but we always had problems getting them done in a timely manner, if at all. After we started setting Rocks, most projects are now completed on time. We've broken everything down into a 90-Day World."

THE 90-DAY WORLD

That leads us to the next point. Why set Rocks every 90 days? We've learned that the human mind tends to lose focus and become distracted after about 90 days into any project. Rock setting gets everyone refocused right on the 90th day as the unraveling begins, maximizing everyone's efforts.

How does it work in practice? Every 90 days you will get together with your team and review the previous Rocks you set to assure they were accomplished. Then you will set new Rocks for the next 90 days. This is called creating a "90-Day World."

In your 90-Day World, you and your team will be focused only on the most important priorities (Rocks) necessary to move the company forward. Everything else—the things that you might like to get done but don't have the capacity or that are just not most important—is pushed to the next 90-day period, minimizing wasted effort, distractions, and taking on too much.

"Before EOS, I would work on a project for a few weeks, and then all of a sudden, my manager would tell me it wasn't a priority anymore, and she would give me a new project. It was very frustrating," said an employee at a paper company in Chicago. "Once we put EOS in place, we keep our priorities for 90 days. All new ideas go on a list for us to talk about when setting our next Rocks."

YOUR ROCKS

Each individual employee should have 1–3 Rocks every 90 days. Your Rocks should be aligned with your company's or manager's Rocks. For example, if one of your manager's Rocks is "Purchase 4 new trucks," your Rock could be "Find 10 potential trucks to buy that match the company's truck specifications" or "Create a standard equipment and inventory list for the new trucks."

A common misunderstanding is that your Rocks are above and beyond your day-to-day responsibilities; that is, they are *extra* work. That is not at all the case. Rocks *are* a crucial part of your job. In addition, sometimes your Rocks will be tied directly to your day-to-day responsibilities. For instance, if you are a salesperson and one of your responsibilities is to schedule sales appointments, one of your Rocks might be "Schedule 20 sales appointments."

At other times, your Rocks won't be tied directly to your day-to-day responsibilities at all; they may have more to do with personal development. For instance, you might have a Rock to take a class, read a book on time management, or help complete a big company project. As long as your Rocks are the most important priorities that you must get done in the next 90 days to help your company or department achieve its vision, you have the right Rocks.

SMART

Another thing about Rocks is that they need to be SMART, which stands for:

- **S**pecific—Is it clear enough so everyone will know when it is completed?
- **M**easurable—Can you measure (typically with a number) the completion of your Rock?
- **A**ttainable—Can you achieve the measurable objective?
- **R**ealistic—Can you complete the Rock in 90 days?
- **T**imely—Is it critical that you complete *this* Rock in the next 90 days? Is this the right time?

Here are some examples of SMART Rocks and those same Rocks *not* written in a SMART way:

Not SMART Rocks	SMART Rocks
Online class	Successfully complete an online training class on website marketing
Requirements for Electrician 2	Pass the requirements (test and field work) for Electrician 2
Safety inspections	Pass 100% of safety inspections
Read a book	Read **What The Heck Is EOS?** and discuss all chapter questions with my manager

The problem with the *not* SMART Rocks is that they are open to interpretation and/or don't have a specific outcome. This will lead to very murky and frustrating conversations when your Rock review is held at the end of the 90 days, which leads to diminished accountability.

For example, take the *not* SMART Rock "Online class." This could mean you registered for a class, you started taking a class, or even that you completed a specific course. However, your manager might interpret this Rock as you having completed an entire semester on marketing. As you can see, making Rocks SMART is essential for creating crystal-clear communication and for setting the right expectations between you and your team.

REVIEWING ROCKS WEEKLY

While Rocks are set every 90 days, you will check in with the team during your weekly meetings. You'll report the status of your rocks by publicly stating to your team if they are "on track" or "off track" (more on this in the next chapter). Your team members will do the same, so you know the status of their Rocks.

Joel Talley of Nexus Health Systems sums up his experience this way: "With Rocks, it is a lot easier to ask people if they got something done. People don't feel called out. Before EOS, it was hard to hold my boss and coworkers accountable. Now I have a way, a language, to hold them accountable—and they don't take it personally or get mad at me when I ask if they got something done. We're all holding each other to a higher level of accountability."

ROCKS VS. MEASURABLES

A final note to avoid any potential confu- sion. In Chapter 2, we mentioned the concept of Measurables—numbers for which you are accountable—and we will discuss this more in Chapter 7. We used examples like number of customer sales meetings, units produced, the days to close the books, on-time shipping, or utilization.

We often are asked, "Can my Rock also be one of my Measurables?" The short answer is yes, provided it is not a gimme. If you have a Measurable that is not consistently being met, it can absolutely be a Rock. Just like the earlier example of the salesperson with the "schedule 20 sales-appointments" Rock, if that person is not hitting their goal, then their Measurable should be a Rock.

Another example of a Measurable becoming a Rock is from Gayco Healthcare, a pharmacy that serves long-term care facilities (e.g., a nursing home). They fill and deliver over 1,000 prescriptions a day. As a result, they need all prescriptions filled by 6:30 PM so they can be delivered on time. The deadline is a Measurable for the team. However, it was consistently *not* being met, so the Rock for the COO was "all prescriptions filled by 6:30 PM every day."

ROCK COMPLETION

On the subject of measuring, you should also realize that the minimum standard for a team's Rock completion is 80%. Expecting 100% Rock completion is perfectionist thinking and dangerous. Why? Perfectionist thinking can lead to teams feeling defeated or being chastised by perfectionist leaders who are only satisfied by achieving perfection (100%). This can also lead to people setting easy rocks so that they can get 100% of them completed.

The objective has then changed from completing the most important objectives to getting all your Rocks done—and this is not the point of Rocks. If you and your team are setting the right Rocks (most important) and then consistently completing a minimum of 80% of them every 90 days, you are doing a great job and outproducing most teams in business.

CHAPTER SUMMARY

When you have successfully created a 90-Day World by setting and completing Rocks every 90 days, you will become more focused, get more accomplished, and have a higher level of accountability.

By making sure your Rocks are SMART, you will have objectives that are specific and measurable so you'll know when they are done. As you complete more and more Rocks, you will experience improved communication, increased self-satisfaction, and more overall enjoyment at work.

As Emmy Georgeson, in recruitment and development at ImageOne, exclaimed, "It's very cool! Just think, we all have about 2 rocks every quarter. Multiply that by 50 team members and then by 4 quarters per year. That's 400 Rocks we accomplish in a year. Those Rocks have helped us move forward in 400 small, manageable steps toward achieving our Vision. Productivity and pride in our work have definitely increased."

Your role is to identify your 1–3 Rocks each quarter, to work with your manager and your team to make sure they are the right Rocks for the next 90 days, and to complete them on time. To help with that, ask your manager the following 3 questions.

Questions to Ask Your Manager

1. When will we start setting Rocks (if you're currently not setting Rocks)?
2. Do you believe my Rocks are the right ones for me?
3. What are your Rocks, and how can I help with them?

CHAPTER 6

WHY DO WE HAVE TO HAVE MEETINGS? (THE WEEKLY MEETING PULSE)

Previously, we would have endless discussions, but decisions never got made—it was very frustrating. With EOS, I love the structured meetings. It really digs to the core of an issue and cuts through the BS.

—DOUG HEBERT, design director, Savage Brands

You've been in them. Meetings that go on and on . . . people talking just so they can hear their own voice . . . decisions that should take 2 minutes end up taking 2 hours . . . Yep, most meetings are a waste of time.

Wait. Let's reconsider that statement for a moment. Actually, meetings are not a waste of time. It's what you *do* in meetings that's a waste of time. If all you do is talk endlessly without solving issues, then yes, you're wasting your time. What if, however, your meetings were productive, helping you solve issues *and* saving you time? Would you feel differently?

Imagine meetings that start on time and end on time. During them you provide input on which issues to tackle, and you participate in the decisions and solutions. You walk out of the meeting with clear resolution on those issues—solving them once and for all with everyone on the same page. Even better, that one meeting eliminates all your other meetings that week. That is what EOS meetings are like.

Let's face it: meetings in business are necessary. The unfortunate reality is that your team can't fully function at its best without productive meetings. The meetings just need to be good meetings. So how do you go about doing that?

END PROCRASTINATION

Most human beings by nature procrastinate; they wait until the last minute to get things done. Here's what normally happens, illustrated by the following procrastination model. You have a meeting (call that point A), and during it, people are usually assigned tasks. The line in the picture below represents the activity to get that stuff done. People delay acting until the last minute—until just before the next meeting at point B—to do everything. You can see the line spike just before the next meeting.

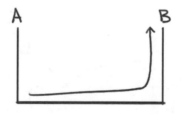

Now, if you only meet once a month, you will only get that spike once a month. Therefore, to the degree you increase the meeting frequency, you create that spike of activity more often, as shown below.

That spike of activity you create looks like an EKG—it is the heartbeat of your organization, or pulse, thus the term "meeting pulse."

WEEKLY MEETING PULSE

We recommend a *weekly* meeting pulse. That way you get a spike of activity 52 times per year (as opposed to 12 times with monthly meetings). By creating that spike of activity more often, you reach a point where there is no time to procrastinate; you come out of the gate running. The activity looks like the picture below.

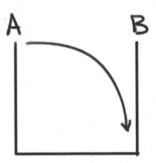

Great organizations minimize the number and length of meetings and maximize meeting productivity. In these organizations, teams have what's called the "right meeting pulse"—the right heartbeat, as mentioned above. Meeting pulse is simply having the right timing and consistent agenda to accomplish 4 things:

1. Make sure everything is on track.
2. Keep the circles connected (stay connected and on the same page with your team).
3. Hold each other accountable.
4. Solve issues.

We've found that the best interval and length of meeting pulse for most teams is to have a 90-minute meeting every week. These meetings are on the same day at the same time, have the same agenda, start on time, and end on time. These meetings are called Level 10 Meetings or "L10" for short.

LEVEL 10 MEETINGS

We call it a Level 10 because when we first meet with a leadership team, we ask them to rate the quality of their meetings on a scale of 1 to 10. They normally give a score of a 4. The following agenda will help you get that rating to a 10.

The L10 is designed to be a time-management tool that actually saves you time by helping the right hand know what the left hand is doing—avoiding train wrecks and bottlenecks that slow things down. And it helps by ending interruptions during the week on issues that can wait to be solved in the meeting. In our experience, you will save 2–3 times the amount of time you spend in the L10 meeting—if you commit to the L10 Agenda.

We'll give you an overview of the L10 Agenda and then describe each section of the meeting. However, before you start, it is important to know 2 things:

1. During this meeting, you will be creating an Issues List. This is the place where you put all the unresolved issues that need to be discussed and solved during the meeting. These are any ideas, opportunities, problems, concerns, or barriers. You'll address these issues during the IDS (Identify, Discuss, Solve) section of the agenda.

2. The meeting must always take place on the same day and at the same time each week. It also must start and end on time. Nothing is more frustrating than a meeting that starts late and runs long. So if your L10 starts at

9:00 AM, get there at 8:55 AM prepared for the meeting. Football coach Vince Lombardi was famous for his mantra that early is on time and on time is late.

Additionally, there are 2 vital roles that make the L10s great. Please make sure someone is accountable for each of these roles in your L10:

1. **MEETING FACILITATOR:** This person runs the meeting. They move the team through the agenda and keep everything on track.

2. **DOCUMENT MANAGER/SCRIBE:** This person manages the documents. They bring the list of Rocks, Scorecard, and L10 Agenda as well as update the L10 Agenda by adding and removing Issues and To-Dos.

The above roles must be assumed by 2 different people, as it is very difficult for one person to play both roles in an L10 meeting.

Below is the Level 10 Meeting Agenda along with an explanation of each agenda item. (Please note the To-Dos and Issues are baked right into the agenda.)

THE LEVEL 10 MEETING AGENDA

Level 10 Weekly Meeting Agenda	
SEGUE	**5 min**
SCORECARD	**5 min**
ROCK REVIEW	**5 min**
CUSTOMER / EMPLOYEE HEADLINES	**5 min**
TO-DO LIST:	**5 min**
• John to Call ABC Co.	
• Bill to have a meeting with Sara	
• Sue to call the supplier	
• Jack to revise core values speech	
IDS:	**60 min**
• Winter sales are down	
• We missed the delivery date on ABC	
• A/R is over 60 days	
• Charles is not following the process	
CONCLUDE:	**5 min**

Notice how the to-dos and issues are built right into the agenda.

SEGUE (GOOD NEWS)

We call this agenda item a "Segue" because that is what it is—an opportunity for your team to transition from your day-to-day battles and to come together to make sure things are on track. In our opinion, the best Segue is to share good news.

During the Segue, each person on the team shares one piece of both personal and professional good news from the past week. Please don't skip this phase or underestimate it. It is a critical part of building a great team and building team health. Sharing good news is a great transition because it helps humanize the process, allows team members to get to know each other better, and starts the meeting off with a positive vibe.

During the next 3 agenda items (Scorecard, Rock Review, and Customer/Employee Headlines), each team member reports what happened that week so that everything important in your area is on track.

SCORECARD

First, you need to make sure your Measurables (Numbers, KPIs, Metrics) are on track and that you're hitting the goals you've set. You review each Measurable as a team and confirm if they are on track or off track. We will cover the Scorecard in more detail in the next chapter.

During the review of the Scorecard, there should be no questions, no color commentary, no excuses. Measurables are either on track or off track—you either hit the goal for the week or you didn't. If a Measurable is off track or if anyone on the team has a question, it gets dropped down to the Issues List. You do this by simply saying, "Drop it down."

Fight the urge to discuss anything during the review of the Scorecard—just report on the numbers. The discussion of numbers that are off track during this part of the agenda turns your meeting into the type of excruciatingly painful reporting session that gives meetings such a bad rap. Avoiding discussions takes a lot of discipline, and it may take your team a few months to really get the hang of it.

ROCK REVIEW

The same as with the Measurables, here you are making sure that each team member's Rocks are on track for the quarter. The person running the meeting (the facilitator) will review the list of Rocks, reading each person's Rock(s) one at a time, and the Rock owner will simply state if it is on track or off track.

Again, that's all you say: "On track," or "Off track." No questions, no color commentary, no excuses. You are either on track to complete your Rock(s) by the end of the 90-day period, or you are not. Any item that is off track or that anyone has a question about gets dropped down to the Issues List.

For example, you might have the Rock to "successfully complete an online web design course." When the facilitator says, "Successfully complete online web design course?" you say, "On track."

Here's where accountability comes into play. Let's say you have a question about a team member's Rock. He says it is on track, but you don't agree or perhaps are a little uncertain. You could ask about it at this point in the meeting, but then what would happen? Twenty minutes later, you'll still be talking about his Rock. Instead you say, "Drop it down," and put it on the Issues List. By discussing it later during the IDS part of the agenda, your team will be in the frame of mind to solve issues.

Practicing this discipline will save you hours of time, eliminate unnecessary discussions, and increase accountability.

CUSTOMER/EMPLOYEE HEADLINES

This 5-minute section allows anyone to bring up good or bad news about customers, employees, or both. These should be quick, 1- to 2-sentence headlines. If it takes more than a sentence or 2 to explain, drop it down to the Issues List.

For example, you might say, "Sheila did a great job on the work plan for ACME, Inc. They are really happy." Alternatively, you might say, "ACME, Inc. is upset about their work plan." Both of these are great examples of Customer/Employee Headlines. In the case of ACME being upset, you would drop it down to the Issues List because it's an issue that needs to be resolved.

TO-DOS

The meeting facilitator will review each To-Do to make sure they are "To-Done." This takes less than 5 minutes. These are the commitments you made to each other in your last L10 meeting. Usually, these are actions you agreed to complete based on how you decided to solve an issue.

For example, let's say your Rock to "successfully complete an online web design course" was off track last week, and it was dropped down to the Issues List. After discussing the ways to get it back on track, your To-Do might have been to select a course by the next L10 meeting. This is the opportunity to confirm your To-Do was done and your Rock is back on track.

To-Dos are typically 7-day action items. The goal is that your team collectively completes 90% of them each week before your next L10. Remember, 100% completion is perfectionist thinking and dangerous.

IDS (IDENTIFY, DISCUSS, SOLVE)

This is the meat of the L10 meeting; this is where the magic happens. This is where you will solve all of your key issues by applying the Issues Solving Track we teach every client. Here, you are going to spend 60 minutes solving issues. You will start by reviewing your Issues List, which you've been building during the first part of the meeting, as well as any issues that carried over from last week's L10. You also want to add any additional issues to the list at this point as well. All issues should be on the list.

There are 3 types of issues on an Issues List:

1. **DECISIONS.** These are issues that need to be solved. For example, Bob is not submitting his reports on time, or customer XYZ is not happy with the level of customer support you've been providing.

2. **INFORMATION TO SHARE.** With these issues, information needs to be shared, such as, "We're having our 2 largest customers into the office this week."

3. **INFORMATION IS NEEDED.** For certain issues, someone needs information to do their job or brainstorming to complete their Rock or project. For example, Roger needs to know when the next software release will be, or Kelly needs ideas for the next marketing campaign.

From the Issues List, pick the top 3 that need to be resolved this week. Once you've identified them (and don't overthink this), start with number 1 and work to clearly identify the real issue.

When number 1 is solved, move to number 2 and then number 3. If you still have time left on the agenda, pick the next 3 most important issues and repeat the process. Your objective is to solve the most important issues well, *not* to solve all the issues on your list. The goal is to solve them once and for all—so they never come back. If you run out of time, the other issues can just stay on the list until next week. Some weeks you will only solve one issue, and other weeks you will solve 10.

IDS'ing

The process you go through to resolve issues is called IDS'ing. IDS is the Issues Solving Track and stands for the following:

- Identify
- Discuss
- Solve

What do those words mean in practical terms?

First, you must **Identify** the real issue before you start to discuss anything. Once the real issue is clearly identified, you then move on to **Discuss**. That's where everyone gives their input on the issue, and once all the views are on the table, you move to **Solve**.

The reason most meetings are a waste of time is that teams spend all their time discussing an issue. They never identify the real root cause, and as a result, they never solve the issue. They just talk and talk and think that they are being productive. That's why you must clearly identify the issue first before discussing it. Then you must understand that the only reason you are discussing the issue is to solve it.

Who, Who, 1-Sentence

To help clearly identify the issue, please use a technique called "Who, Who, 1-Sentence." It works like this:

- **WHO.** The first "who" is deciding who is raising the issue.
- **WHO.** The second "who" is understanding who is ultimately accountable for solving the issue.
- **1-SENTENCE.** This means that the person raising the issue must look the person who is accountable for the issue in the eye and state the issue in one sentence—short, sweet, and to the point. No candy-coating.

This is sometimes hard to do, so let's look at an example from a customer-service L10 meeting.

FACILITATOR: Who is teeing this issue up?
BOB: I am.
FACILITATOR: Who are you talking to?
BOB: Sue.
FACILITATOR: What's the issue in one sentence?
BOB: Sue, I'm not getting reports from you on time.

This is exactly what the process should be like. From here, you can have a productive conversation that might go like this:

SUE: Huh? What are you talking about?

BOB: My customer reports. I need them daily, but I only get them every other day at best. I can't answer my customers' questions if I don't have the most recent reports.

FACILITATOR: I'm not sure we've identified the real issue here. Sue, any idea why Bob is not getting the reports on time?

SUE: Bob, I didn't know you needed them daily. I think that is the real issue. Now that I know, I can send them to you by 9:00 AM every day. Will that work?

BOB: That would be great.

SUE: I'll take a To-Do to start sending them to you. We can check next week in our L10 and make sure that is working for Bob.

BOB: Great. Thanks, Sue.

FACILITATOR: That issue is solved. On to the next issue. Who's teeing up the next issue?

Imagine if solving a problem was actually that easy. Well, the truth is, it can be with a little practice. We see it every day. As one employee said, "Getting to the real issue was hard, because a lot of times, it was about people. IDS'ing helped us to identify issues and solve them without people taking it personally. I was really surprised."

Tangent Alert

Important note: Beware of the tangents that exist in most unproductive meetings. That is when people start getting off the subject and going down rabbit holes.

For example, a team starts talking about increasing sales, and 5 tangents later, they are discussing the company letterhead. The conversation goes like this: "Sales are down; we need to increase sales." Then someone brings up the salespeople and what they're doing, and from there they start to discuss one salesperson, Victoria. That subject leads to that of Victoria and Jack in accounting not getting along. This leads to the question, "Did Jack send the letter to customers who still owe us money and are past due?" which raises the question, "Did he use the new letterhead?"

You don't have to sit there helplessly. When this starts to happen, do what we teach every client. Simply say, "Tangent Alert!" This is a great way to alert your team to the fact that the conversation has started to go sideways and needs to be brought back to the original issue.

Another fun trick is to just say "Rabbit!" to humorously let the team know that they are going down a rabbit hole.

One last note on IDS'ing: Try to resolve issues at your department level and avoid kicking them upstairs as much as possible. One of the reasons your leadership team is implementing EOS is to give you the autonomy to resolve issues at your team level—to empower you to fix the things you see and they don't.

CONCLUDE

With 5 minutes left in the meeting, stop whatever you are doing—even if you are in the middle of an issue. Because you still need to do 3 things and end the meeting on time:

1. **RECAP THE TO-DO LIST THAT CAME OUT OF THE MEETING.** Review each item to make sure everyone is clear on and committed to their To-Dos.

2. **DECIDE IF THERE ARE ANY CASCADING MESSAGES.** These are important messages to communicate to others inside or outside the company based on the decisions you've made. You quickly decide who is going to tell the others, what they are going to tell them, and how they are going to tell them.

3. **RATE THE MEETING.** Everyone rates the quality of the meeting on a scale of 1 to 10, with 10 being the best. Ask, "So, how did we do today?" and everyone provides their rating.

When rating the meeting, think about the following criteria:

1. Did it start and end on time?
2. Did you follow the L10 Agenda?
3. Is everyone on the same page?
4. Did 90% or more of the To-Dos get done?
5. Did you solve the most important issues?

Rating the meeting will help you self-correct and improve. The minimum average rating for your L10 should be 8. If a team member rates the meeting below an 8, ask, "What would have made the meeting a 10 for you?" The answer will provide you with ideas on how to improve.

If you and your team meet the above 5 criteria, the L10 will save you time, increase accountability, and make you more productive. You'll also find that the L10 will usually replace almost every other meeting.

For a tutorial video on the L10 Meeting, go to https://traction.eosworldwide.com/level-10.

Most, but not all, teams need 90 minutes each week. You might find that you complete the L10 Agenda and solve all your issues in 30 or 60 minutes—great! You'll figure this out as you go forward, but start with 90 minutes scheduled for the L10—you can always end the meeting early. But if you consistently finish the meeting in 45 minutes, for instance, then hold a 45-minute departmental L10 every week.

CHAPTER SUMMARY

Once you are up and running with L10s, communication, accountability, and results will improve. Everyone will become more aware of what everyone else is doing. By practicing the Issues Solving Track and IDS'ing with the "Who, Who, 1-Sentence" technique, you'll solve issues quickly—once and for all, so they never reappear.

Lisa Fisher from United Paint summarized her experience this way: "Before the L10s, *UGH!* We jumped from topic to topic with no real agenda, with lots of complaining and finger-pointing. I would leave these meetings sometimes and ask myself: What was the purpose of that meeting? Did we actually solve anything? There was no real accountability.

"Since the weekly L10 meetings, there is less off-topic complaining and he said/she said discussion. There is an agenda every meeting and clear accountability for actions that were agreed to from the previous week's meeting. Issues actually get discussed with defined actions to solve them."

Doug Hebert from Savage Brands added, "The L10 is not personal. It's the one place we can say what needs to be said. I look forward to the meeting. It's the highlight of my week."

Your role is to participate in your L10s. By participate, we mean bring issues to the meeting, be open and honest when discussing issues, fight for the greater good of the team, and hold yourself and the team accountable on Scorecard Measurables, Rocks, and To-Dos. To help with that, ask your manager the following 3 questions.

Questions to Ask Your Manager

1. Will I be punished for bringing up any issues in the L10?
2. Will you get mad if I give the meeting a low score?
3. Can we watch the L10 Video at https://traction.eosworldwide.com/level-10 and discuss how we can improve our L10?

CHAPTER 7
WHAT'S MY NUMBER?
(SCORECARD & MEASURABLES)

After we started using Scorecards, everyone on the
team knew exactly what our goals were and what
each person would be measured on. It made it easy
to identify areas of the business that were performing
well and areas that were underperforming. We can
quickly change areas that are underperforming
before they turn into a huge problem.
—BRAD SOVINE, eCommerce, Uckele

Imagine yourself playing a sport and you can't see
the scoreboard. You don't know the score; the
referees will not tell you when you commit a foul
or penalty; you don't know how much time is left

on the clock. You're not sure if you're winning or losing, and the frustrated coach tells you, "Just play harder."

We know that sounds crazy, yet that is how a lot of companies operate. No one knows what the targets are or how they are doing in terms of achieving those targets—they don't know if they are winning or losing. They are just working hard. This results in wasted time, poor resource allocation, weak overall performance, and ultimately, terrible results. Just like playing that awkward sport, the people in the company have no idea how they are doing and, as a result, perform poorly—or, at a minimum, are frustrated, confused, unmotivated, and rudderless.

In contrast, imagine a workplace where you know exactly how you, your department, and your company are doing. Your key numbers are tracked weekly, so as a group you have an absolute pulse on what's being done. You know the score. Everyone has a number and consistently hits their targets. And if a number is ever off track, you IDS it to get it back on track. Accountability is high because everyone can see how they are doing.

What we just described may sound like utopia to you, but it's not. It is absolutely possible, and the way you create it is to use a Scorecard.

A Scorecard contains a handful of numbers that tell you how your company or department is doing. It will tell you what is working and what is not, helping you identify and solve issues before they become major disasters. The Scorecard will save you time by removing the guesswork and eliminating assumptions, emotions, and egos from your day-to-day conversations.

As Emmy Georgeson in recruitment and development at ImageOne said, "It's great to see a snapshot of the most important numbers that help us know where we are and how we're improving (or slipping!). Measuring and sharing the numbers creates transparency and visibility, and makes us all feel like we're contributing to the big picture. It is 'real'— not some lofty, pie-in-the-sky document. Rather, this is how it is. Let's celebrate, or let's get going and make these numbers better!"

DESIGNING THE SCORECARD

You may have heard terms like Dashboard, Flash Report, Pulse Report, KPI, or Metrics—they're all the same concept. We prefer the term Scorecard. A typical *company* Scorecard will have 5–15 numbers that your leadership team reviews every week. Each department should have a *department* Scorecard. That Scorecard will usually have 3–5 numbers that you should review weekly in your L10.

The numbers on a Scorecard (whether company or department) most often are activity-based leading indicators, meaning they measure current activity that produces future results. Some examples:

- Utilization
- Units Shipped
- Number of Sales Appointments
- Website Visits
- Accounts Receivable Balance
- Number of Customer-Service Problems
- Average Time to Resolve Complaints

Each of these describes the activity of an individual or department that will produce future results like revenue, sales, and profit. For example, you might have a company goal to achieve $10 million in revenue, and as a result you need to schedule 20 sales appointments per week to hit that goal. The logic is, 20 sales appointments leads to 5 new clients, which leads to $200,000 in sales per week, which leads to $10 million in annual revenue. The 20 scheduled appointments is the activity-based leading indicator, and the $10 million in revenue is the future result.

Below are 2 examples of department Scorecards using activity-based numbers.

SALES DEPARTMENT SCORECARD								
Who	Measurable	Goal	3-Mar	10-Mar	17-Mar	....	26-May
Laurie	# New Leads						
Okan	Total Opportunities in $						
Ron	# Scheduled Sales Appointments						
Lliam	Win Rate %						

OPERATIONS DEPARTMENT SCORECARD								
Who	Measurable	Goal	3-Mar	10-Mar	17-Mar	....	26-May
Sue	% Utilization						
Jennifer	% Service Level						
Jon	$ Cost per Unit						
Paul	# Overtime Hours						

A Scorecard must have 4 key columns: Who, Measurables, Goal, and Date.

- "Who" is the person accountable for the number.
- "Measurables" are the 3–5 numbers you are tracking weekly on your Scorecard.
- "Goal" is the number that must be hit every week.
- "Date" is the week on which you are reporting.

A further note on the "Who": this is the person responsible for hitting the weekly goal. It is *not* the person with the easiest access to the number but, instead, the person who can most influence the number to hit the weekly goal. For example, your manager may have access to the weekly units shipped report, but you actually ship the units. In this case, you would own this Measurable.

You might have noticed that the examples have room for 13 weeks of results. Scorecards must display 13 weeks of data at a glance. By seeing 13 weeks of results, you can identify patterns and trends, potentially identifying issues before they negatively impact your results. It will also help you identify chronic issues such as service levels missing their goal for 10 of the past 13 weeks. If that happens, we

encourage you to really dig deep to find the underlying issue.

A Scorecard requires hard work, discipline, and
consistency to manage, but it's worth the effort.
You'll know where you are relative to your goals,
and you can course correct if you're off track. Alternatively, you can celebrate the week when you blow
your number out of the water.

To make a Scorecard work, only one person
should take responsibility for it, making sure it is
completely accurate. Typically, this is the department leader, but not always.

WHAT GETS MEASURED GETS DONE

By implementing a departmental Scorecard, you
will see instant results because the truth is, what gets
measured gets done. In Dale Carnegie's book *How to
Win Friends & Influence People*, he provides a powerful
example of this.

Charles Schwab (no, not the financial institution)
ran Bethlehem Steel Company in the early 1900s,

and he had a mill that wasn't producing good results. Schwab asked the mill manager what was going on, and the manager said he had tried everything.

Since this conversation took place at the end of the day, Schwab asked the manager for a piece of chalk and asked the nearest man how many heats (i.e., batches of refined steel) his shift had made that day. The man said 6. Without another word, Schwab chalked a big, white "6" in the middle of the floor and walked away.

When the night shift came in, they saw the "6" and asked what it meant. The day people explained that Charles Schwab, the big boss, had asked how many heats they'd made and chalked the number on the floor. The next morning, Schwab walked through the mill again and he found that the night shift had rubbed out the "6" and replaced it with a big "7."

When the day shift reported to work, they saw the "7" and decided they would show the night shift a thing or two. The crew pitched in with enthusiasm, and when they quit that night, they left behind an enormous "10." It wasn't long before this mill was outproducing every other plant.

These are the kind of results you can expect from a Scorecard. Once you have solid results at your fingertips, you gain a pulse on your business and the ability to predict. This will naturally lead to the opportunity for every employee to have a single, meaningful, manageable number to guide them in their work.

EVERYONE HAVING A NUMBER

Those 3–5 numbers of the Scorecard naturally become the numbers for each person on your team. For example, the sales numbers become each salesperson's numbers. The operation numbers become each operation person's numbers. If your team has a goal of "Scheduling 20 meetings a week" and there are 5 salespeople, then each one may be accountable for "Scheduling 4 meetings a week." That is their number. This ultimately leads to what we call "Everyone Has a Number."

When EOS is fully implemented in your company, each person should have a Measurable or number for which they are accountable. Why should every employee have a number? Let's look at 8 reasons.

1. **NUMBERS CUT THROUGH MURKY SUBJECTIVE COMMUNICATION BETWEEN MANAGER AND EMPLOYEE.** As an example, the old response between a sales manager and salesperson regarding last week's sales activity might be a vague "Great!" A number-based answer, such as "I got 3," creates more clarity. If 3 is the goal, then great. However, if the company needed 10, there is an issue to solve.

2. **NUMBERS CREATE ACCOUNTABILITY.** When you have a number, everyone knows what the expectation is. All accountability begins with clear expectations, and nothing is clearer than a number.

3. **ACCOUNTABLE PEOPLE APPRECIATE NUMBERS.** Wrong People in the Wrong Seats usually resist Measurables. The Right People in the Right Seats love the clarity of knowing the numbers they need to hit, and enjoy being part of a culture where all are held accountable. They know if they are winning the game.

4. **NUMBERS CREATE CLARITY AND COMMITMENT.** When someone is clear on their number and agrees that they can achieve it, you have commitment.

5. **NUMBERS CREATE COMPETITION.** In the earlier example, Charles Schwab was able to create competition by making the target known to all teams. Sure, they might experience some discomfort and a little stress, but there is nothing wrong with a little pressure.

6. **NUMBERS PRODUCE RESULTS.** Simply put, what gets watched improves.

7. **NUMBERS CREATE TEAMWORK.** When a team of the Right People in the Right Seats agree to hit a number, they ask themselves, "How can we hit it?" creating camaraderie and peer pressure. Those who don't pull their weight will be called out by their team members.

8. **NUMBERS SOLVE PROBLEMS FASTER.** When an activity-based number is off track,

you can attack it and solve the problem proactively.

A marketing employee at one organization provides this insight as to the value of Measurables: "Marketing is hard to measure. People always thought my area was just a waste of money. Now they can see what I accomplish, and they value marketing."

Having a number also allows you and everyone else to objectively see how you are doing. And your number will provide you clarity on how you are progressing toward your longer-term goals.

CHAPTER SUMMARY

With your departmental Scorecard in place, being reviewed weekly in your L10 meeting, and everyone in your organization having a number, you'll know exactly how you and everyone else is doing. You'll identify and solve issues more quickly, averting catastrophes. Performance will improve because you'll know exactly what needs to get done to hit your targets and win.

Keith Klevenski, systems engineer at Accudata, stated, "The weekly review of our Scorecard and Measurables allows for the proactive correction of issues. Everyone is paying attention to the same numbers, and it is helping us achieve our goals."

Your role is to review your department's Scorecard each week in your L10 and help IDS any numbers that are off track. Your role is also to know your specific Measurable and to consistently hit it.

To help you with that, ask your manager the following 3 questions.

Questions to Ask Your Manager

1. Does our department Scorecard contain the right numbers and goals?
2. Is this a good Measurable for me? (Bring 2–3 suggestions.)
3. What is your Measurable, and how do I help you hit it?

CHAPTER 8
HOW AM I DOING?
(PEOPLE ANALYZER)

The best tool is the People Analyzer. It made
the biggest impact and helped us identify
the Right People for the Right Seats.
—**KELLY IMHOFF, marketing, Staley, Inc.**

People Analyzer might sound a little scary—maybe even a little cold. Actually, it's really not. In fact, after working with thousands of managers, we can tell you that, at first, your manager was probably a little apprehensive as well. Really, how many times have you heard a manager say, "I can't wait to analyze my employees"?

This tool has a higher purpose. Great organizations are built by having the Right People in the Right Seats—100% across the organization—and that's what the People Analyzer helps you do. In Chapter 2, we defined the Right People as people who fit in your company's culture. These people act according to your company's Core Values.

In Chapter 4, we defined seats using the Accountability Chart. The Right Seat means placing everyone in a role where they can best contribute to the organization. This is the job where their innate talents and skills are put to the best use. Each seat is defined by an average of 5 roles and responsibilities as shown below:

Customer Service
John
- Solve customer issues
- Document customer interactions
- Escalate when appropriate
- Open and close customer accounts
- Generate sales leads

The People Analyzer is a simple tool that pulls Core Values and the Accountability Chart together and helps your organization identify if they have the Right People in the Right Seats. As Doug Hebert puts it, "The People Analyzer was a real eye-opener for me. It is really clear when people don't align with our Core Values or fit their role—it's just not their [thing]."

So how does it work?

STEP 1

On the People Analyzer you list a person in the left-hand column and then your company's Core Values across the top, as shown:

THE PEOPLE ANALYZER™

Name	Be Humbly Confident	Grow or Die	Help First	Do the Right Thing	Do What You Say	
Sally Jones						

The person is rated on how they live or don't live your company's Core Values with a plus, a plus/minus, or a minus. Here are the definitions for each rating:

- A plus (+) means that they live the Core Value most of the time. No one is perfect.
- A plus/minus (+/-) means that sometimes they do and sometimes they don't live the Core Value. They're hot and cold.
- A minus (-) means that most of the time they do not live the Core Value.

When completed, the People Analyzer might look like this example:

THE PEOPLE ANALYZER™						
Name	Be Humbly Confident	Grow or Die	Help First	Do the Right Thing	Do What You Say	
Sally Jones	+	+	+	+	+	
The Bar	+	+	+	+/-	+/-	

Every company sets a minimum standard, or "The Bar," for the People Analyzer. You will notice it listed at the bottom of the People Analyzer. This is the minimum score a company will accept from the People Analyzer. If you have 5 Core Values, our recommended Bar is any combination of 3 "+'s" and 2 "+/-'s."

STEP 2

The next step is to determine if each person is in the Right Seat. Using the Accountability Chart, each person is evaluated against their seat's roles and responsibilities using 3 criteria called "GWC." This stands for:

1. **GET IT:** Do they "get" the job?
   - Do they understand all the ins and outs of the position?
   - Do they understand how their job relates to and affects others?
   - Do all the neurons in their brain connect for that job?
   - A flight attendant who's rude or a salesperson who doesn't understand the product after months of training are examples of people who don't "Get It."

2. **WANT IT:** Do they "want" the job?
   - Do they genuinely want to do the job?
   - Do they get up every morning wanting to do it?
   - Do they show passion for it?
   - For example, at a family business in Texas, the accounts receivable clerk told her manager, "I've been doing this for 10 years. I really would like to do something else. I guess I just don't want this seat anymore."

3. **CAPACITY:** Do they have the "capacity" to do the job?
   - Do they have the emotional, intellectual, and physical ability as well as the time to do the job?
   - A receptionist who can't work the phone system or a pest-control field rep who is scared of bugs are 2 examples of people who don't have the capacity for their seats.

The answer to each GWC question is a yes or a no. Either they Get It, Want It, and have the Capacity to Do It, or they don't. There are no maybes. When those 3 columns are added, the completed People Analyzer will look like this example:

Name	Be Humbly Confident	Grow or Die	Help First	Do the Right Thing	Do What You Say	Get it	Want it	Capacity to Do It	
THE PEOPLE ANALYZER™									
Sally Jones	+	+	+	+	+	Y	Y	Y	
The Bar	+	+	+	+/-	+/-	Y	Y	Y	

The minimum standard, or "The Bar," for GWC is 3 yeses. The People Analyzer will now show a complete picture of whether your company has the Right Person in the Right Seat. The above example shows that Sally is the Right Person in the Right Seat.

STEP 3

The next step is to apply it to yourself. That will give you a very clear answer of whether you are the Right Person in the Right Seat. Here's how to do it:

1. On the following diagram, fill in your company's Core Values across the top followed by Get It, Want It, Capacity to Do It.
2. Fill in your name in the far-left column.

3. Give yourself a +, +/-, or - for each Core Value based on your honest assessment of how well you live that specific Core Value.
4. Give yourself a yes or no for Get It, Want It, and Capacity to Do It.
5. Compare yourself to your company's Bar.
6. Note: In order for this to be a useful tool, you need to be completely open and honest with yourself about how you live your company's Core Values and if you GWC your current seat.

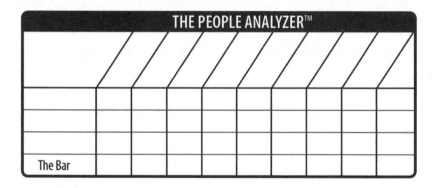

WRONG FIT—DON'T PANIC

Once you see the results, don't worry. If you're the wrong person, it doesn't mean you are a bad person. It only means you might be a better fit in a different company culture. If you're in the wrong seat, it just means you need to find a seat that better fits your talents and skills—a seat where you can be more successful.

As an employee in a professional services firm on the West Coast said, "I was in the wrong seat and failing. It sucked and it was affecting my personal life. I finally got into the Right Seat, and I'm much more successful—and a lot happier."

THE QUARTERLY CONVERSATION

At this point, you're probably wondering, "How did my manager complete this 'thing' on me?" Since your company is using EOS as its operating system, you'll have a chance to find out. And this leads us to the Quarterly Conversation.

Imagine being able to sit down with your manager every 90 days and have a real, open, and honest discussion about how you are doing—about what's working and what's not. Most employees we've talked with would love more feedback and opportunities to discuss how they're doing with their manager.

That's why we teach every manager to have Quarterly Conversations with their direct reports. So, hopefully, you are already having them with your manager. If not, you should request them.

The Quarterly Conversation is just that, a conversation. It is not a formal performance review; there is no documentation, but it is okay for you and your manager to bring notes. In fact, for your first Quarterly Conversation you might want to bring your People Analyzer and compare notes with your manager. Remember 2 things, though:

1. Notes are to help you prepare for the conversation, not to document it.
2. Your manager is probably just as nervous as you are.

The Quarterly Conversation is an informal, face-to-face, one-on-one meeting for you both to talk about what's working and what's not. It takes about 60 minutes. This dialogue should be a 2-way street—an opportunity for you both to clarify expectations, to communicate well, to keep the circles connected, and if necessary, to make course corrections.

A Quarterly Conversation, taking place every 90 days, works because, as we mentioned in Chapter 5, human beings tend to lose focus and fray around that point. Meeting at 90-day intervals with your manager is a great way to reset for the next 90 days.

When preparing for your Quarterly Conversation, focus on 2 topics: "What's Working" and "What's Not." Here are some questions to ask yourself when preparing for the "What's Working" discussion:

- What am I most proud of accomplishing in the last quarter?
- What changes did I make to better accomplish my job?
- What did I do well to hit my Rocks and Measurable(s)?
- Am I working on projects and in a role that really matters?
- How have I demonstrated the company's Core Values?
- Did my manager provide the necessary tools and direction to do my job well?

When you start preparing for the "What's Not Working" discussion, it is important to understand that this is *not* meant to be a blame session. You are identifying issues that you can work on with your manager to resolve. Also, please keep in mind that everyone has aspects of the job that are "not working"—it just makes us normal human beings. Here are some questions that may help you prepare:

- What makes my job more difficult?
- What processes and procedures are broken?
- Have I identified the root cause of any issues I'm having?
- What could I have done differently in the last quarter?
- How have I not demonstrated the company's Core Values?
- What could I have done differently to hit my Rocks and Measurable(s) (if you missed any)?
- How could my manager have helped me be more successful?
- What's not working for your manager? (If you don't know, ask.)

We're often asked how Quarterly Conversations fit with Annual Performance Reviews. The Quarterly Conversations should complement the Annual Performance Review by keeping you in the loop regarding your performance. A good or bad Annual Performance Review should never be a surprise—if you and your manager are doing a good job of keeping the circles connected.

A final note: please don't wait for your manager to come to you. If you don't have a Quarterly Conversation set on your calendar with your manager, go to them and ask them when would be a good time to start.

CHAPTER SUMMARY

When your company has implemented the People Analyzer, you'll reach a point where you have 100% of the Right People in the Right Seats. Work will get done more efficiently, and mistakes will be rare. Communication will improve, and expectations between managers and employees will be crystal clear. The company will function like a well-oiled machine, consistently hitting and surpassing targets. Your role is to evaluate yourself, openly and honestly, using the People Analyzer. To help with that, ask your manager the following 3 questions.

Questions to Ask Your Manager

1. What was your analysis of me, using the People Analyzer?
2. When will we start having Quarterly Conversations?
3. What do you think is working and what is not?

CHAPTER 9

WHAT DO I DO NEXT?
(CONCLUSION)

Overall, I love EOS and the impact it has had on my team and myself. If I'm ever in a different company, I'll be implementing EOS to help the team work well together and achieve higher results.

—JORDAN-ANN SCHORCH,
accounts, Syrup Marketing

Congratulations! You're nearly to the end, so let's quickly recap what you've learned. Your company chose EOS as its operating system. Your company's goal is to become 100% strong in each of the 6 Key Components: Vision, People, Data, Issues, Process, and Traction.

When you are 100% strong, everyone will be rowing in the same direction and aligned around the same short-term and long-term goals documented in the V/TO.

There will be less chaos and fewer fires to fight. Thanks to the Core Values, Accountability Chart, and People Analyzer, everyone will be the Right Person in the Right Seat, with clearly defined roles and responsibilities, making decisions faster and solving issues more quickly, propelling your organization forward. Everyone will be following your Core Processes, creating consistency and the ability to grow.

Using Scorecards and Measurables, everyone will know how they are doing against their targets. You'll be living in a 90-Day World setting and completing Rocks every 90 days. Meetings will be productive as a result of the L10, and you'll be solving all your issues by IDS'ing.

You will be winning and having fun.

You now have all the tools you need and know the role you're expected to play to help achieve that 100% strong goal. Remember: your manager asked you to read this book because they want you to take an active role in achieving your company's vision.

As stated earlier, implementing EOS in your company is an ongoing, lifelong effort, and many companies have been running on EOS for more than 10 years. EOS has had a positive impact on the lives of millions. As one employee said, "EOS has had a large effect on me personally. I have discovered that this simple process can be carried over into my personal life as well. It has given me tools to gain progress in areas where my life goals were merely just maybe-someday wishes."

ORGANIZATIONAL CHECKUP

Finally, to help you determine how your company is doing running on EOS, complete the following short organizational checkup. You can also go to www .eosworldwide.com to fill out this organizational checkup online.

For each statement below, please rank your company on a scale of 1 to 5, where 1 is weak (or you don't do it) and 5 is strong (you're very good at it).

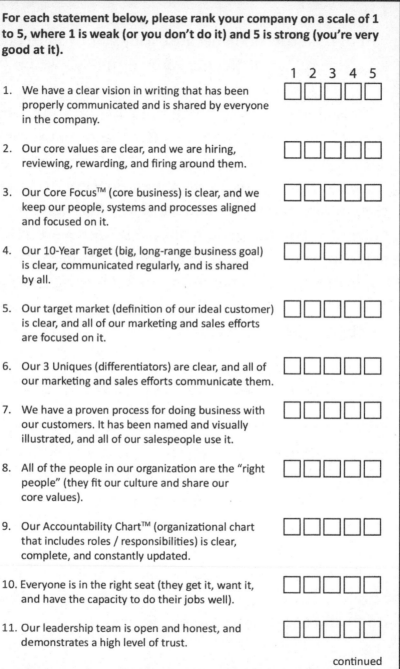

THE EOS ORGANIZATIONAL CHECKUP ™

For each statement below, please rank your company on a scale of 1 to 5, where 1 is weak (or you don't do it) and 5 is strong (you're very good at it).

1 2 3 4 5

1. We have a clear vision in writing that has been properly communicated and is shared by everyone in the company.

2. Our core values are clear, and we are hiring, reviewing, rewarding, and firing around them.

3. Our Core Focus™ (core business) is clear, and we keep our people, systems and processes aligned and focused on it.

4. Our 10-Year Target (big, long-range business goal) is clear, communicated regularly, and is shared by all.

5. Our target market (definition of our ideal customer) is clear, and all of our marketing and sales efforts are focused on it.

6. Our 3 Uniques (differentiators) are clear, and all of our marketing and sales efforts communicate them.

7. We have a proven process for doing business with our customers. It has been named and visually illustrated, and all of our salespeople use it.

8. All of the people in our organization are the "right people" (they fit our culture and share our core values).

9. Our Accountability Chart™ (organizational chart that includes roles / responsibilities) is clear, complete, and constantly updated.

10. Everyone is in the right seat (they get it, want it, and have the capacity to do their jobs well).

11. Our leadership team is open and honest, and demonstrates a high level of trust.

continued

THE EOS ORGANIZATIONAL CHECKUP ™

	1	2	3	4	5

12. Everyone has Rocks (1 to 7 priorities per quarter) and is focused on them. □ □ □ □ □

13. Everyone is engaged in regular weekly meetings. □ □ □ □ □

14. All meetings are on the same day and at the same time each week, have the same agenda, start on time, and end on time. □ □ □ □ □

15. All teams clearly identify, discuss, and solve issues for the long-term greater good of the company. □ □ □ □ □

16. Our Core Processes are documented, simplified, and followed by all to consistently produce the results we want. □ □ □ □ □

17. We have systems for receiving regular feedback from customers and employees, so we always know their level of satisfaction. □ □ □ □ □

18. A Scorecard for tracking weekly metrics/ measurables is in place. □ □ □ □ □

19. Everyone in the organization has at least one number they are accountable for keeping on track each week. □ □ □ □ □

20. We have a budget and are monitoring it regularly (e.g., monthly or quarterly). □ □ □ □ □

Total number of each ranking [ ] [ ] [ ] [ ] [ ]

Multiply by the number above   x1   x2   x3   x4   x5
[ ] [ ] [ ] [ ] [ ]

Add all five numbers to determine the percentage score that refelects the current state of your company: [ ] %

Total your score by adding together all the numbers in the last row. This is your starting score. Your company's goal is to get a score above 80.

Most companies score below 80 when they are getting started with EOS. If your score was below 80, don't worry—that's normal. Your leadership team is working hard to get above 80 and they can't do it without you. To help, we recommend you review and act on the role you're expected to play. Also, ask your manager the questions listed at the end of each chapter. There is a concise summary of your role and the questions to ask your manager in Appendixes A and B.

EOS AND YOU

In reality, your company cannot become 100% strong in all 6 Key Components and run well on EOS without you.

What we are trying to say can be summed up in this short story. Near a little village in the center of Turkey, an old, wise man lived up on a mountain in a cave. From time to time, the villagers would go seek his counsel, and the old, wise man always had the answer. Some people tried to outsmart him, but they never could—he always had the right answer.

Meanwhile, 2 boys from the village who craved fame and glory devised a plan to finally outsmart the old, wise man. They would catch a small bird and cup it in their hands. The boys would ask the old, wise man, "Is the bird in our hands dead or alive?"

If the old, wise man said, "Dead," the boys would open their hands and the live bird would fly away. If the old, wise man said, "Alive," the boys would smash their hands together and show him a dead bird. Their plan couldn't fail, and they would soon be known worldwide as the boys who had outsmarted the old, wise man.

After catching a small bird, the boys put their plan in action and hiked up the mountain to the old, wise man's cave. "Sir," they said, "is the bird in our hands dead or alive?"

The old, wise man paused and thought for a while. After a few minutes had passed, he replied, "The answer is in your hands."

And the same is true for you. If you're sitting back wondering if EOS will work or not, the answer is in your hands.

APPENDIX A:
YOUR ROLE

Each chapter ended with a definition of the role you are expected to play regarding EOS in your company. Here is a short summary of those roles:

- Understand and believe in your company's Vision (answers to the 8 V/TO questions).
- Align all your efforts toward helping achieve that Vision.
- Know where you fit in your company's Accountability Chart.
- Understand and fulfill the responsibilities of your role.
- Identify your 1–3 quarterly Rocks, working with your manager and your team to make sure they are the right Rocks for the next 90 days, and complete them.

- Participate in your L10s, bringing issues to the meeting, being open when discussing issues, fighting for the greater good of the team, and holding yourself and the team accountable on Measurables, Rocks, and To-Dos.
- Review your department's Scorecard each week in your L10 and help IDS any numbers that are off track.
- Know your specific Measurable and consistently hit it.
- Evaluate yourself honestly, using the People Analyzer.

Appendix B:
Questions to Ask Your Manager

To help you actively engage in the above roles, we gave you questions to ask your manager. Here is a recap of those questions:

Chapter 2. The EOS Model Questions

1. What is our weakest component, and how can I help strengthen it?
2. What is our strongest component, and why do you think that?
3. What is the first thing you want me to do to help implement EOS at our company?

Chapter 3. The Vision/Traction Organizer (V/TO) Questions

1. How can our department help achieve the company Vision?
2. What role do I play in achieving the Vision?
3. What is our greatest challenge in achieving our Vision?

Chapter 4. The Accountability Chart Questions

1. What seat am I in, and what are my 5 roles and responsibilities?
2. Am I in the Right Seat where I can contribute the most to the organization?
3. What are your 5 roles and/or responsibilities, and how can I help you?

Chapter 5. The Rock Questions

1. When will we start setting Rocks (if you're currently not setting Rocks)?
2. Do you believe my Rocks are the right ones for me?

3. What are your Rocks, and how can I help with them?

Chapter 6. The Weekly Meeting Pulse Questions

1. Will I be punished for bringing up any issues in the L10?
2. Will you get mad if I give the meeting a low score?
3. Can we watch the L10 Video at https://traction.eosworldwide.com/level-10 and discuss how we can improve our L10?

Chapter 7. The Scorecard and Measurables Questions

1. Does our department Scorecard contain the right numbers and goals?
2. Is this a good Measurable for me? (Bring 2–3 suggestions.)
3. What is your Measurable, and how do I help you hit it?

Chapter 8. The People Analyzer Questions

1. What was your analysis of me, using the People Analyzer?
2. When will we start having Quarterly Conversations?
3. What do you think is working and what is not?

APPENDIX C:
EOS TERMS

We've used a lot of new terms, so here is a summary of them and where you can find them best defined in the book:

ACKNOWLEDGMENTS

This book would not have been possible without the help and guidance of the following people. We will never be able to thank you enough for your impact on our lives, our work, and this book.

GINO'S FAMILY, FRIENDS, MENTORS, AND TEACHERS

Kathy, my strong and beautiful wife. I could not do what I do without your support. I appreciate you and love you with all of my heart.

Alexis, my incredible daughter. You are as beautiful on the inside as you are on the outside. You make me so unbelievably proud and make me smile every day.

Gino, my quick-witted son. You are an engineer with a personality. Thank you for always making me laugh. I am so incredibly proud of you.

Linda Wickman, my mom. Thank you for your quiet strength, your wisdom, and your inspiration. You always make me feel so loved. I think about you every day and love you very much.

Floyd Wickman, my dad and life mentor. Thank you for everything you taught me about leading and managing people; it changed my life. You are the entrepreneur's entrepreneur. Thank you for the inspiration for The People Analyzer and A Simplified Business Plan.

Sam Cupp, my business mentor. Thank you for meeting with me every month for all of those years. You turned me into a businessman. Since your passing, there isn't a day that goes by that I don't miss you. Thank you for the inspiration for the Scorecard.

Karen Grooms, the world's greatest business manager. You keep me in my Unique Ability® and protect me from the world. Thanks for over twenty years of holding all the pieces together.

Don Tinney, the best business partner a guy could have and an EOS Implementer extraordinaire. Thank you for proving it is possible that someone other than me can be an EOS Implementer. What a ride it has been.

Tom Bouwer, my co-author and one of our best EOS Implementers. You made writing this book an absolute pleasure. You have so many amazing gifts. Thanks for your commitment to the EOS cause.

EOS Worldwide Leadership Team (Mike Paton, Amber Baird, Lisa Hofmann, Tyler Smith, Marisa Smith, Kelly Knight, and CJ Dube). Thank you for running the company like a Swiss watch so that I can continue to create content for the entrepreneurial world.

Dan Sullivan. Thank you for helping me discover my Unique Ability® and showing me how to build a life around it. You have made a great impact on my life. You are truly the coach of all coaches.

Verne Harnish. Thank you for being a pioneer, for inviting me into your world, and for showing me that there is a place out there for my craft. Thank you for your passion and the impact you have had on the entrepreneurial world. Your teachings have inspired me.

Jim Collins. Thank you for your amazing work, research, and inspiration. Your research on Core Values, Core Purpose, putting the Right People in the Right Seats, and proving that "Level 5 Leaders" have a place in the world has simplified my work. You have truly changed the course of business history.

My clients. Thank you for over 1,700 full-day sessions of enabling me to do what I love. Thank you for the risks you take, your passion, your incredible hard work, and the many lives you impact.

TOM'S FAMILY, FRIENDS, MENTORS, AND TEACHERS

Sevilay, my amazing, strong, and resilient wife. I could not do what I do without your help, support, and advice. *Teşekkür ederim. Seni seviyorum.*

John Bouwer, my father. I'm so lucky to have you as an example. Thank you for the many opportunities, for making me listen to Peter Drucker cassettes on long family car rides, and for charging me 8% interest on a $300 loan when I was 12. You taught me to never stop learning and developed in me a passion for business. I would not be who I am without you.

Marian Bouwer, my mother. Thank you for the musical talent and passion you shared with me—it has taken me all over the world and made my life that much richer. It is from you that I learned the gift of giving.

Alex Freytag, my amazing business partner and mind-blowing EOS Implementer. I could not have asked for a better partner and match. Thank you for taking this journey with me, for introducing me to EOS and other new ideas, for pushing me, for our Clarity Trips™, for your calming guidance, and for your passion for learning.

Jenna Spencer, our marvelous former assistant. You are such an amazing person. You kept Alex and me on track in our early days and then had the guts to start your own company. Every day you impact thousands of people.

Becky Pearson, our remarkable assistant. Thank you for stepping into Jenna's impossible-to-fill shoes and seamlessly filling them 100%. You have no idea how much we rely on you or how incredibly easy you make our lives.

Gino Wickman, my co-author and business sage. Thank you for taking the risk and struggling through the hard years to create EOS and our community. You have given me The EOS Life. I learn from you every time we talk and you made writing this book an outright joy.

The Honey Badgers, my tribe. Thank you for your love, your open and honest conversations, and for always pushing me to reach a higher standard on this path to mastery.

The EOS Implementer Community. Thank you for allowing me to be part of such an amazing community. I've learned from each and every one of you.

Mocha, Boo Boo, Tiffany, Scooby. Thank you for your unconditional love, for all we've shared in the past and will share in the future, and for making me a better person.

My clients. For your faith in me that enables me to do what I love and for the opportunity to work with and learn from you—I love every session we have together.

CONTRIBUTORS

Story Contributors: Erin Cassidy, Lindsey Clement, Theresa Denaro, Myra Ebarb, Marcia Faschingbauer, Lisa Fisher, Emmy Georgeson, Doug Hebert, Danielle Hicks, Kelly Imhoff, Keith Klevenski, Jon Martin, Jacob Martinez, Sarah McNulty, Bill Patsiga, Brian Pirkle, Kevin Polachowski, Curt Rager, Jordan-Ann Schorch, Brad Sovine, Joel Talley, and Kathleen Watts.

The Manuscript Readers: Walt Brown, Lindsey Clement, Ellyn Davidson, Theresa Denaro, Rob Dube, Myra Ebarb, Lisa Fisher, Alex Freytag, Emmy Georgeson, Rick Gordon, Doug Hebert, Danielle Hicks, Kelly Imhoff, Keith Klevenski, Dave Laming, Beth Lenz, Jennifer Lockhart, Sarah McNulty, Chris Naylor, Becky Pearson, Kevin Polachowski, Ed Pryor, Rachel Rys, Todd Sachse, Jordan-Ann Schorch, Susan Sisson, Brad Sovine, Jenna Spencer, Joel Talley,

Kathleen Watts, and Jill Young. Thank you for your time and hard work.

Other Contributors: Our literary agent, Matthew Carnicelli of Carnicelli Literary Services; our editor, John Paine of John Paine Editorial Services; our illustrator, Drew Robinson of Spork Design; and our publisher, Glenn Yeffeth, and the team at BenBella Books.

About the Authors

GINO WICKMAN, bestselling author of *Traction*, has a passion for helping people get what they want from their businesses. To fulfill that passion, he created the Entrepreneurial Operating System® (EOS), which helps leaders run better businesses, get better control, have better life balance, and gain more traction—with the entire organization advancing together as a cohesive team. Wickman is the founder of EOS Worldwide, a growing organization of successful entrepreneurs collaborating as certified EOS Implementers to help people experience all the organizational and personal benefits of implementing EOS. He also delivers workshops and keynote addresses.

THOMAS J. BOUWER has a passion for helping entrepreneurs and their leadership teams simplify, clarify, and achieve their vision. In addition to starting and running three of his own companies in Turkey, Tom has worked with a diverse range of companies, from start-ups to Fortune 50 companies. His nearly three decades of global management and consulting experience in multiple industries help him quickly identify and solve chronic issues that keep a company from achieving optimal success. As a teacher, facilitator, and coach, Tom spends most of his time as a Certified EOS Implementer—helping leadership teams implement EOS in their companies. He earned his B.A. from Hope College and MBA from the Fuqua School of Business at Duke University. When not delivering EOS workshops or keynote addresses, Tom is most likely walking his dogs or hiking in the mountains.